Making It in Manhattan

The Beginner's Guide to Surviving & Thriving in the World of Fashion

CAROLINE VAZZANA

Skyhorse Publishing

Skyhorse Publishing books may be purchased in bulk at special discounts for sales promotion, corporate gifts, fund-raising, or educational purposes. Special editions can also be created to specifications. For details, contact the Special Sales Department, Skyhorse Publishing, 307 West 36th Street, 11th Floor, New York, NY 10018 or info@skyhorsepublishing.com.

Skyhorse® and Skyhorse Publishing® are registered trademarks of Skyhorse Publishing, Inc.®, a Delaware corporation.

Visit our website at www.skyhorsepublishing.com.

10 9 8 7 6 5 4 3 2 1

Library of Congress Cataloging-in-Publication Data is available on file.

Cover design by Jenny Zemanek
Cover illustration by Mats Meyer, matsmeyerillustrations.com

Print ISBN: 978-1-5107-3202-5
Ebook ISBN: 978-1-5107-3203-2

Printed in China

To my mom & dad,

thank you for always believing in me.

TABLE OF CONTENTS

Making It in Manhattan

Introduction

DEAR READER

Take a front row seat as I guide you through the ins and outs of the fashion industry. From a very young age, I knew I was meant to work in a creative field. (Well, after I realized that being a princess wasn't really an option.) Once I finally set my heart on fashion, I wanted to learn everything I could about the industry, from the many career paths, other than just a buyer or designer, to really mastering how to get your foot in the door. Today, this might seem pretty easy with social media and being able to look up everything on the Internet, but back then I didn't have all of the resources available to us today, so I had to think outside the box.

As I got older and learned more about the inner workings of the fashion industry (well, watched movies and TV shows about it), I wished and dreamed of what working in New York City and the world of fashion would be like. Unfortunately, though, life isn't always like the movies (surprise, surprise), and landing an interview or ultimately your dream job won't just be given to you by a magical fairy godmother—I'm looking at you, Cinderella.

Gaining access to such an amazing and thrilling industry in the city that literally never sleeps takes countless hours of hard work and dedication. Here, I'm shedding some light on my story and pulling back the curtain on what seems to be a mysterious industry. Everyone has their own story as to how they found their calling and what prompted them to listen, but

I believe it's what you do during your own journey that truly matters and will ultimately lead you down the right path. My hope is that my journey will inspire you to follow your own calling of breaking into the fashion industry and making it in Manhattan.

Chapter 1

THE *ART* OF FASHION

Growing up, I was surrounded by a family of doctors, so I was sort of the odd ball out. Now, I'm not saying this in a bad way at all! I mean, someone has to be the unicorn of the family, right? While my siblings focused on math and science projects during our childhood, I was usually in my room coloring pictures, cutting up old dresses I owned, and sewing them into different outfits. I never realized that people could actually  make a career out of something so fun and creative, and it wasn't until a few years had passed and many drawings later that I did.

I'll never forget the day I found out there was more to art than my stacks of coloring books and 64-count pack of crayons. I was ten years old and went to a private school where your skirt couldn't rise above your knee and socks had to be folded over once (they actually checked). Though my school may not have seemed the most creative on the outside, the highlight of my entire week was my one-hour art class. Each week we were given something new to draw. In the particular class I'm referring to, we had to draw a cowboy. Since this was my favorite class, I often took too much time focusing on the little details of the picture and couldn't finish in time.

My art teacher, Mrs. Klein, gave me permission to work on my cowboy at home and bring it to her the next day. (My obsession with color and attention to detail started early, as you can tell.)

My older sister and I both had a soccer game after school that day, so my mom picked us up and drove us over to the field, decked out in our shin guards and cleats. (So chic!) On the way to the game, though, I took out my picture and continued working on it. I remember thinking I did a great job and that my cowboy looked like Woody from *Toy Story*. (Who doesn't love a classic?) The next day I happily arrived at school and put my picture under Mrs. Klein's door, eager to hear what she thought.

One week later when we finally had art class again, Mrs. Klein started out the period by walking around handing out our artwork, each with a grade on the back. I sat in my desk very content, knowing in my mind I probably did well. (The key to life is confidence.) When I got my picture back, though, all that was written on the reverse side was "See me after class." *Gulp!* My heart started to quiver and my palms started to sweat. Oh no, did I do something wrong? Did she not like my work? Maybe I got detention! All of these and many more thoughts raced through my ten-year-old mind. Well, forty minutes later, a sweaty little nervous girl walked up to her teacher's desk. I hesitantly asked, "You wanted to see me?" Voice trembling. Mrs. Klein looked at me with a warm smile and said, "Oh yes, your picture is very good."

I couldn't believe it, was something I did actually that special that it needed this much attention? Mrs. Klein proceeded to tell me that my art skills were above those of someone my age and that I should look into taking after-school private art lessons with her if I'd be interested. My heart leapt with joy, I couldn't believe it. But before I could give her a decision, I rushed home to ask my mom; I was only ten, after all. My mom was so proud and said I could, of course, do the lessons if I wanted to. From that moment me to fashion editorial.

Now, I know what you're thinking, *Your life must be like The Devil Wears Prada*. If only I had a quarter every time someone asked me if my life was like that movie, and to that question my answer is no—most of the time. Of course, in life you'll run into the difficult Miranda Priestleys of the world, but if you're lucky you'll also run into the Nigels, who are kind and inspiring. (If you don't remember who Nigel was, he was Andy's co-worker who gave her that incredible makeover—I mean, remember those Chanel boots?!)

Anyhoo, as I worked my way up and into editorial, I simultaneously got to work my way into the most exciting events in Man-hattan, including what some might refer to as the holy grail of the fashion world: New York fashion week (NYFW). Having only seen fashion shows in movies like *Sex and the City* and *The Devil Wears Prada*, of course I was more than excited—I was ready. I was ready to learn everything there was to know about this magical time of year and this enchanted world, a world where you can walk in wearing your trusty old ballet flats and leave wearing Manolos. (And never want to take them off!) Fashion week, on top of the energy and excitement, comes with many emotions and leaves you utterly drained by the very last day, when you sadly must return to reality. It is a time when we can escape from our regular lives and experience what fashion can really do, bringing so many people together for a common cause. It might seem as though attending fashion week were all fun and games, but it actually takes a lot of trial and error, many a regrettable outfit (speaking from personal experience here!), and a few little white lies to get that coveted front row seat.

Chapter 3

IT'S ALL ABOUT THE INTERNSHIPS

In my opinion, the one thing that's just as important as graduating from college, if you're hoping to enter the fashion world, is landing an internship (or two) before you actually walk on that stage come graduation day. An internship, like it did for me, can ultimately help you figure out what you want to do with your life. Hey—if it hadn't been for my internships, I probably never would have figured out what I wanted to do after I threw in the towel on being a designer.

Maybe your heart is set on working in editorial as mine was on design, but it won't be until you've had your first internship and really experienced working in a fashion closet that you will know if this is for you. Internships are a vital part of any industry (not only fashion) and can really help you land a job down the road. There is nothing more valuable than hands-on experience to help affirm (or disaffirm) your "dream job."

Back when I was applying for my first internship, social media wasn't what it is now and my resources were very limited. If I were applying for an internship today, though, my two go-to sources would be Ed2010.com and Fashionista.com. These two sites are always posting current, up-to-date positions just waiting to be filled. Not only are these companies looking for interns immediately, all postings also have a direct company contact. Yes, you heard that correctly, you don't have to apply through a website and send your résumé and cover letter to what feels like a dead end or down a black hole. I wish I had known about these sites when I was applying for my first internship because it would have made my life much, much easier. In regard to social media, it's more than just a fun platform to upload pictures, it's a business in itself; remember this at a young age so you don't have to go back and delete hundreds of embarrassing selfies or pictures from a crazy night out that you don't want your future em-

ployer to see. I would suggest posting fashion-related content such as your outfits, a new pair of shoes you bought, or your favorite look from a recent collection in case a future employer should look at your page. You always want your social media presence to reflect the best version of you.

Stay current in social media trends and events by creating a professional LinkedIn profile or an Instagram. LinkedIn, in particular, is an incredible job resource, so take advantage of it. It's a platform that is strictly for widening your network and building a professional profile. It allows you to list your past and current job experiences, what kinds of jobs you are looking for in the future, and even a recommendation or two to round out your profile. You have access to almost every industry insider right at your fingertips on LinkedIn. It's easy to look up companies you might want to intern or work for and send a message to a few of their employees to ask for an informational interview: a chance to invite them for coffee and ask them a few questions about their career. When sending a message on LinkedIn or another social media outlet, keep it simple and sweet and definitely not too personal. The worst thing they can say is no, and at that point at least you will know you tried.

How to Ask for an Informational Interview

Dear Mr./Ms. **(insert last name here)**,

I hope all is well. My name is **(insert name here),** *and I am currently a* **(insert your grade here)** *at* **(insert your college or high school here)**. *I am* *extremely interested in one day pursuing a career in the fashion industry and truly admire your career at **(insert company here)**. I was wondering if you might be willing to meet for coffee so I could ask you a few questions about your career and gain some insight into the fashion industry.*

Thank you in advance for your time and consideration.

Sincerely/All my best,
(insert signature here)

> One time, I was speaking to an underclassman in college who was looking to land a job in graphic design after graduation. He came across a job opening at one of his favorite companies, so I told him how to apply and who to email. A few weeks later, I ran into him when I was up at his college speaking on a fashion panel and asked if he had actually sent out the emails and if he had heard anything back. He told me he didn't because he was nervous and felt awkward emailing the person and possibly leaving a bad impression with the company. When he told me this, another panelist, who had overheard our conversation, quickly chimed in and asked him, "Well, do you work at (insert company name here) now?" The boy of course responded, "No, I don't." The panelist, who is creative director for a major public relations (PR) firm, then quickly told the boy something to the effect of, "Well if you don't work there now you won't be any worse off by emailing them, you have nothing to lose." This is SO true, you have nothing to lose by reaching out and just inquiring about an opening. The worst that can happen is one of two things: one, they might just not answer, or two, they might answer and tell you that you aren't the right fit for the company. Either way, you will not be any worse off than you were before; the only thing that might change is you could actually land the job of your dreams!

Once you do finally land your first internship, work extremely hard and be willing to do anything and everything. Whether it is getting coffee for your boss or making copies of a document, always say yes. When you do a good job with the more menial tasks, eventually you will be trusted with the big stuff. Working hard and forming a good relationship with your internship coordinator or boss really pays off in the long run. Not only can this person be a reference when applying for jobs or write you a stellar letter of recommendation, they can also serve as your mentor, someone to turn to throughout your career for guidance and advice. A person like this can honestly make or break your career and is simply invaluable.

> *Networking and building relationships not only with your boss but also your fellow interns are extremely important. You never know where someone might end up five years down the road, so it's always good to keep in touch. During my first internship, I was given the opportunity to attend a conference for fashion interns in New York. At this conference I did my best to network and build as many connections as I could. From that conference I landed another small internship and actually made a few friends. Fast-forward several years, and I am still friends with the girls I met so many years ago at that conference. They all moved to New York and work in fashion, as well. This industry is such a small world, so it's important to always be kind to others. You never know when you may run into them again!*

Chapter 4

HOW TO NETWORK ON INSTAGRAM

Unlike LinkedIn, Instagram can right off the bat feel a bit more informal. Since everyone is posting images of themselves and even going live via Instagram stories, etc., it can make you feel like you already know someone you admire. Because of this, I often get asked the question Can you network on Instagram? And to this, my answer is a resounding *Yes*, if it is done properly. Instagram is a great connector. It can easily connect you with people you look up to in the fashion industry, people you may not normally be able to access so easily. For those of you in high school or college and not in New York City, Instagram can be a great way to feel connected to the industry. For me, I love staying connected with designers and editors and being able to instantly see what's going on in the industry.

If there is someone whose career you admire, first things first, before you send them any sort of message, make sure to follow them (not literally). From there, engage in their content to help them become familiar with your page or even your icon so that when you message them it doesn't seem out of the blue. From there, send them a direct message or an email if it's listed on their profile. Today, many people have their email listed on Instagram so you won't have to actually slide into their DMs (direct messages). Either way, I would send them some variation of the message I suggested for LinkedIn (pg. 10). Since Instagram isn't strictly for networking, I suggest jazzing up the message a bit by discussing why you admire their career and how it aligns with your past experiences or goals in the industry. The more passionate you come across in your message, the more likely they are to answer.

Chapter 5

How to Build a Successful Brand Using Social Media

As you are all well aware, social media isn't going anywhere. The digital age we live in is getting stronger each and every day. Now more than ever it's so important to use social media for your benefit. There's no reason you shouldn't be making money or building your brand awareness via the various social channels you scroll through on a daily basis. Not sure where to start? Neither did I. When Instagram first came out, I was in the middle of my first internship in NYC. I was pretty technologically challenged at the time, but thankfully the other interns I worked with urged me to download this new app called Instagram and showed me how to use it.

At that time, I didn't really think that one app could have an impact on the fashion industry, and me, in such a huge way. Fast-forward several years and several jobs later, I decided to leave my full-time nine-to-five job and become my own boss. A huge part of what I wanted to accomplish was creating a strong personal brand across all of my social media channels. Yes, I know this sounds overwhelming, but it's not as bad as you might think, and once you start, it all really becomes second nature.

Here, I'm sharing a few things I've learned along the way to help you build your own social media presence and start using it to further your own brand and maybe even make some money.

CONSISTENCY IS KEY

If I've learned one thing, it's that we as humans are creatures of habit. We like knowing what's going to come, so posting content every single day around the same time is really important. Your followers want to know they can come to your page every day and see something new, so posting consistent content will help you gain as well as maintain your follower base. Personally, I like to stick to fashion and beauty content that is all centered around New York City and shows a lot of color. Once you create a theme, stick to it so people know what to expect.

DEVELOP A SCHEDULE

Creating some sort of series or special hashtag that is unique to your page gives your followers something to look forward to. Whether it's a #TuesdayShoesday post every week or a #WhatsOnMyDeskWednesday series as I've started, something that is weekly will draw in viewers because they know they can expect to see it each and every week.

KEEP COLORS COHESIVE

Are your pictures faded and light or are they super bright and vibrant? Personally, my color scheme is very bright, and I keep my pictures saturated. I love color, so I really play that up on my page. For the most part, it's important to edit your pictures the same way every time so your page looks uniform. Think of your social media like you're telling the story of your day-to-day life and all of the pages need to look as though they were from the same book.

Be Yourself

Everyone else is taken, so you might as well be yourself. Yes, it is totally okay to draw inspiration from larger accounts (I mean, who doesn't?), but at the end of the day, do your best to be completely unique and true to who you are.

Build Your Partnerships

The best way to build your social media presence is through collaborations with brands and larger accounts. The more you can reach a larger audience, the more likely you are to build your own follower base. However, just because you are partnering with a certain brand, never alter your own voice or style to fit in better with the brand. Try your best to partner with brands that are already "on brand" to who you are. If a brand reaches out and wants to work with you, it's because they already like you and feel like your brand complements theirs, so never feel pressured to change to fit in.

Who Are You?

What is your style? What is your brand? What can you bring to the conversation that isn't already being said? Once you can answer those questions, you can really start building your brand. There are obviously so many people out there to follow, so it's important to think, Well, *why me*? Why should someone follow me? Whether your focus is beauty, career, fashion, or lifestyle, figure that out and stick with it. And don't be discouraged, the answer to this question doesn't often come overnight. This is something that took me several years to figure out, and in some ways, every day I am evolving and growing, so who I am is always changing. But try your best to find a base. For me, I can confidently say I have a colorful and eclectic sense of style and my goal through my brand is to lend career advice to the future fashion generation in a fun and informative way. I've tried my best to create colorful and approachable social platforms so that my followers always feel comfortable reaching out to me and asking for advice.

ALIGN EVERYTHING

Managing a wide range of platforms from Snapchat to Instagram to Twitter, Facebook, Pinterest, YouTube, and a blog can make social media consistency quite challenging. This is why your very first step before posting content should really be to figure out your style, voice, and message. Really take time to figure out what you want to present to the world, because once you do, that is what will set you apart and make you unique in an oversaturated market. And believe me, it all gets easier with time, and once you know who you are and what your message is, you will never second-guess yourself again before hitting the "share" button.

supermodel or celebrity standing outside of the venue and were dressed in what was probably some of the most beautiful clothing I had seen at this point in my life.

Our tickets were for standing room, so when we walked inside of Lincoln Center, we were greeted with a long line. People who work in the industry are usually always given a seat, so when there are no more seats, they give out standing room tickets in the back. Standing room tickets are a necessary part of Fashion Week, though. After months and months of hard work and preparation, designers want their shows to be completely full, so the standing room people can help fill any seats left vacant come show time.

When we finally made our way inside the venue, it all felt so surreal. The theater was dark, and the only real light was at the end of the runway where the designer's name was lit up on a beautiful backdrop. Standing there and looking at the designer's name—the designer I had worked with all summer—felt incredible and just so magical. There I was standing at my very

first fashion week. I could honestly say I had worked with this designer, and the feeling was indescribable. After just standing there in shock and disbelief and taking it all in for a few minutes, we finally made our way to the standing room section.

It's nice to have a seat at fashion week because you can, of course, see the clothing better, take better pictures, and you also might receive a gift bag.

Every seat at my first show had a gift bag with an adorable floral pattern on it. I was hoping that somehow the seats would not fill up and I would be seated among all of the people who actually work in the industry (wishful thinking, to say the least). As the minutes passed, the seats were filling up, and it looked as though I might not get a seat after all (sigh). Suddenly, I heard the chime of my name from a familiar voice. My internship coordinator was at the show and was happy to see me. She immediately came over and ushered us, the former intern crew, to empty seats. I couldn't believe it, my first fashion week and I actually got a seat (and a good one, I might add)! As we sat down only a few rows away from the runway, I felt like I was in a dream, a dream I never wanted to wake from. Sitting across the way from us was a group of girls in the front row wearing flower crowns. They looked *so* cool and I remember thinking, *Who are those girls? I want to be like them!* Everyone was gathering around and taking pictures, so I figured it must be someone important. It turned out to be Alexa Chung, one of my now-style icons, go figure.

As the lights started to dim and the music began to play, the show was beginning. As I watched garments float up and down the runway, my excitement grew even further (if that was even possible), when I began to actually recognize pieces I had worked on during my summer internship. The feeling of belonging and knowing I had a small hand in making this show possible was truly indescribable, and something I will never forget. With that being said, there was no time to celebrate because this made me want to work even harder and reach even further, because I knew I still had a long way to go.

Chapter 7

PUT IN WORK

Returning to reality and back to college after my first fashion week at Lincoln Center, I knew I wanted and needed more. I was eager to continue learning about all of the different aspects of the industry and just knew I had to be part of it all again, no matter what I had to do. On that note, I decided to ask my internship coordinator from the summer, whom I had recently seen at the show in September, if she needed any help during the next fashion week that would take place in February. I knew I was emailing her way in advance since September fashion week had just ended, but I was very eager and wanted to make sure no one beat me to the punch. When asking a company if they need help during one of the most exciting and busiest times in the industry, the answer is usually always yes (if the spots haven't already filled up, of course).

> Once you've had that first internship, make sure to keep in touch with your boss. Maintaining a good connection with your past employer is key. Periodically email them and ask them how they are doing. If you see something exciting in the news about your old company, reach out with your congratulations. It's important not to come across as too eager, which I'm sure we have all done at one time or another, but sending follow-up emails every now and again helps you to stay fresh in their minds should an exciting opportunity arise. So, to intern with them again during fashion week (or any other time really), just shoot your past employer an email and express your

interest. Tell them how much you valued your past experience and how you would love to come back and help out again in any way needed. Volunteering to work fashion week is one of the easiest ways to get in without a ticket! If you haven't had an internship but are still looking to volunteer at fashion week, you may be asking yourself, **How can** *I* **do this?** To that *I* say, take advantage of your resources. LinkedIn, Twitter, Instagram, as well as the fashion internship sites *I* previously mentioned (pg. 5). Though the above may seem like fun and personal social media outlets, there are many designers who check their pages regularly as well as editors. Send them a short but sweet message about how you would love to volunteer your time. They might write you back that they are not looking for help right at this moment, but they may know someone else who is and will keep you in mind should something open up. Everyone knows everyone in the industry; *I'm* not exaggerating. The fashion industry is honestly like a spider web. Editors are always speaking to PR people, who are then speaking to designers, etc. As one person meets another person, that person meets another and tells that person about you. (*I* know it sounds confusing; just think of it like Dominos how each one taps the other in a never-ending cycle). Through these connections, the fashion "web" is honestly a very small and tight-knit one. Once you land your first internship or make that first connection, the people now in your web can introduce you to others and pass your information along, thus growing your own personal web.

During fashion week, the designers and their teams are under a lot of pressure and usually more than happy to take on help (no one says no to *free* help!). I wanted to highlight the word *free* here because your time will (most likely) not be paid. You will be volunteering your time out of the goodness of your heart and for your love of fashion. Just remember that and try not to get discouraged over not being paid right away.

> *Your first few experiences in the fashion industry will most likely be unpaid. In exchange for your hours of hard work, you might be receiving school credit, a clothing allowance (if you're lucky), or most important, invaluable experience. This can be tough when starting out since everything in Manhattan is so expensive. To help fill your empty wallet, I would suggest getting a part-time job on the days you aren't interning so you can save up some money.*

Before I knew it, the leaves were changing, the snow began to fall, and it was finally almost time for February fashion week. Once February came, I ventured back to New York City for two weeks and took an absence from class, again. (Oopsie!) Thankfully, most of my professors were super understanding. You gotta do what you gotta do!

Instead of working in production, where I worked during my summer internship, I was placed in a different department. For fashion week, I was going to be in the pattern-making department where the garments were actually made, so my daily tasks were as follows:

- Sew buttons onto all and any garments that needed, making sure they were tight and reinforced.

- Sew trims onto garments.

- Lint role everything prior to the show.

- Clean the shoes for the models.

- Run garments back and forth around the city when needed.

I think you get the idea. I pretty much did everything and anything to help prepare the collection for the show—and I loved every single minute of it.

Plus, I now knew how to sew a pretty mean button, which still comes in handy, I might add!

When I interned there in the summer, things were a lot more laid back and nothing was as urgent. Now, I was getting to experience a whole other side of the company: not only was it fashion week, but especially since I was in a different department that was more hands-on and technical, I was able to learn more of what goes into the small details of making a garment. I honestly learned so much in those two short weeks and would definitely do it all over again, even though I was a bit sleep deprived by the end. But who wouldn't be? It's fashion week, after all.

The day of the show, I arrived at work extra early because I could hardly contain my excitement. I was at my workstation just looking over everything when I was told the designer a.k.a. the Big Boss (you know, the one whose name is on the tag) needed to see me. It turned out she didn't like how one of the garments looked on the hanger and wanted someone to try it on for her. Thankfully, I was the same size as the fit model, and I was more than happy to help try on the garment. Seeing her the day of the show was very interesting. She was extremely calm, super sweet, and told me the dress looked great on me. She must have been confident in the collection, which is always a good thing. I was definitely expecting her to be a bit more panic-stricken or something, but it was a nice surprise to see her as the exact opposite.

Arriving at work early and staying late never hurts. I was so happy to get some one-on-one face time with the designer of the company, but if I hadn't arrived at work early I would have missed a great opportunity to not only spend time with her, but to do so on the day of the show!

After that minifitting, I was allowed to actually go down to the sample room and pick out any dress I wanted to wear for the day of the show. I picked this green floral dress, which I was allowed to later keep and continue to wear all the time. The day of the show flew by faster than shoppers running into the Manolo Blahnik sample sale! Her show started at six, but I had to head over to Lincoln Center at around two. I was told that I was going to be one of the interns bringing the collection over to the venue, but I wasn't given details on what exactly that would entail.

When two in the afternoon rolled around, I was handed several large garment bags and told to take the subway uptown to Lincoln Center with another intern and enter the building through the back door. I was in shock; we were taking the new collection on the subway? With the fate of the show in my hands, I was sure something was going to go horribly wrong.

The other intern and myself left right away with the collection overflowing in our arms. This part depended on us; if we messed up, the whole show would be ruined. Yikes, boy was I nervous. On the subway, I hung my garment bag hangers from the overhead bar, hoping the clothing wouldn't get wrinkled. I received many questioning looks as well as actual questions. My favorite was "Are you a designer going to show your collection?" Ha, I wish! I was more like one of Santa's very happy, eager, and anxious elves helping deliver toys.

When we got to Lincoln Center, I was unsure where the back entrance was since I had only been there once in the fall, and even that time I got lost. Finally, after asking a few security guards, we found it but were greeted by a long line of others trying to get in, as well. I assumed since we had the collection, though, we would have been able to cut the line and go straight in, right? Wrong. We waited in the line for twenty minutes or so before we got to the front. Then when we did, the security guard was wary of letting us in! There I was, holding the collection that needed to be walking down the runway in just a few hours in my arms, pleading with this security guard to let us in. It wasn't a pretty picture. After several minutes of going back and forth, he finally saw it my way and cleared us to enter. Disaster averted!

> Talking to fashion week security is different from talking to any other person. Being extremely nice and friendly is key. Who knows, if you make friends with a security guard, they could possibly sneak you backstage or into a few shows! When all else fails, though, just be persistent and don't take no for an answer. In life, no is rarely ever the final answer, so learning that from a young age is key. When you get a no from one person, take it as an opportunity to try a different tactic or pursue something else. I don't only mean this when bartering with fashion week security, either. When applying for jobs or even asking for a promotion, no is never the final answer. When you receive a no, most of the time no just means not right now. For example, say you apply for a job at your dream company and you get rejected. Well, in a year or two you will have much more experience and many more connections. Who knows? That same person that told you no the first time might tell you yes the second! Also, being nice to everyone in life will get you far. Whether it's the CEO of the company or the doorman, be kind and always have a positive attitude. As they say, you catch more bees with honey than you do with vinegar, so always be the "honey" of your group.

Chapter 7 | Put In Work

As I walked through the doors backstage, I realized I was now seeing fashion week from a whole new perspective and it *definitely* looked different. You could feel the tension and sense of urgency in everything that was happening backstage; it was such an adrenaline rush. I finally entered our section and started unpacking the collection; we made it without a scratch, which I really couldn't believe—*Let the internal happy dance begin!* But it wasn't show time just yet, so there was no time to celebrate our seamless journey there until later. After I unpacked and hung up the collection, the models started coming in and getting their hair and makeup done. It was all so surreal and I felt like I was watching a movie. My boss then gave me a badge to show I was with the team in case anyone else (I'm looking at you, security guard) gave me any trouble for being backstage. How could this be real? Someone pinch me! My whole life I had dreamed of attending fashion week, and this alone beat all of my expectations. Nothing is like seeing fashion week from the eyes of the designers and the team who has put countless hours and nights into these mere fifteen (or so) minutes. Fashion shows are actually extremely short compared to what you might expect. Design teams work tirelessly for months and months for such a minute amount of time, so it's extremely important that everything go by without a hitch.

The models now had their hair set in rollers and their makeup done, and the designer wanted them to do a practice walk on the runway. She had decided she wanted three of the models to do a little dance step before they started to walk, so she really wanted to see them practice it before they did it live in front of a full theater. We were all invited to sit in the dress rehearsal while they practiced this dance step and walk down the runway. I of course wanted to watch, so I went out into the empty theater, and when I looked around I was honestly speechless (a rarity for me). Standing in this huge empty theater with just the designer and models was extremely rewarding and made all of my hard work those past few weeks more than worth it. I stood there and reflected on it all, my internship last summer, attending fashion week for the first time last fall, and now here I was backstage watching the magic of how it all happens come to life. I started to get choked up thinking about it all. As the music began and the three models started to do the step, it was so surreal. I mean, how many people can say they got to see Karlie Kloss in her early days in a special preshow rehearsal? Oh, did I mention that the model leading the dance routine was Karlie Kloss? One of my favorite models? It was all so special and really such a dream come true. The dress rehearsal went seamlessly, and the designer was thrilled as she cheered the girls on and off the runway. She was so fun and laid back, which made the entire experience even more enjoyable for everyone on her team. As soon as we finished the dress rehearsal, we all ran backstage and quickly got all of the girls into their first looks.

With two minutes until show time, everything was ready, and my boss came up to me and told me to go pick any empty seat in the house so I could enjoy the show. I was thrilled to hear she wanted me to go in and watch because honestly I was really hoping to get to actually see the show as it all came to life. I was able to find an empty seat (with a gift bag!) right in the second row. Just a few months ago, I was hoping to get any seat, and now I was told to take my pick—this was a dream I never wanted to wake up from. As the lights dimmed and the music began, Karlie came out to begin the show. As the models walked on and off the runway, I saw the buttons I had sewn, the clothing I had steamed, and the shoes I had shined. I felt so unbelievably proud to be even just a small part of this show. Everything I had done, all of my work, was right there in front of me. As the show ended, I gathered my things and headed backstage.

Backstage I was on cloud nine, and I was greeted by the other interns who were fawning in the corner over some model I had (at the time) never heard of. They were all huge fans but were all too nervous to go over and say hello, so I decided to! I think I was still running on a high from seeing the show because that took a lot of courage for little old me at the time.

I headed over and introduced myself, and we started chatting and ultimately took a picture. She was so unbelievably nice and everyone was in awe of how I just strolled over, introduced myself, and asked for a picture. The model turned out to be Cara Delevingne!

> *Fake it until you make it! No one needs to know you don't know who they are or how to properly pronounce Christian Louboutin. Always play it cool and be kind, that goes a long way. In the case of fashion week, if you are attending a show for the first time, you might want to do a bit of research. What models usually work for this designer? What celebrities are usually seen wearing their clothes? It helps to know these things. Should you be lucky enough to rub shoulders with one of these people, you will be able to easily start a conversation and make a good impression. Who knows, with shows flooded with editors, bloggers, and designers, your next boss could be closer than you think.*

As I left the venue and headed to the subway, I was reeling. I still couldn't believe all that had happened in this one day. I sat down on the subway and began reading over the program, which was on all of the seats of the theater. On the last page of the program, there was a special thank-you page. As I skimmed down the list of names, my heart stopped beating, I couldn't believe it—MY NAME WAS IN THE PROGRAM. As I sat there and stared at it for a solid ten minutes, all I could think was, this is only the beginning.

Chapter 8

IS THE BEST-DRESSED LIST UP?

When it comes to dressing for fashion week, things are a bit different. As opposed to dressing for any average day of work, fashion week is a time where you really want to show your own individual style and possibly even take a few risks. For this one week, you really get to push the limits and wear something bold or extravagant. That bright multicolored dress you feel is a bit too loud for the office? Perfect! When faced with bloggers, editors, and stylists, you'll want to make sure you fit in (or stand out) and make a good impression during this time of year. A good way to know what to wear is to do some research. Look at street style pictures from the previous seasons. And this doesn't only apply to fashion week; whenever I attend a major gala or larger scale event I've never been to before, I always do my research to see what attendees have worn in the previous years. This also works well when it comes to interviews. Say you land an interview at a major company but are unsure what to wear, try doing a little digging/snooping/research online to see if you can find any hints about their office style so you never have to show up to an event (or interview!) and feel out of place—one of my many tricks!

As far as fashion week goes, though, things have probably changed since that last fashion week and new trends have formed and other trends have taken more of a backseat, but just getting a feel of the atmosphere and what it is actually like is important and will help you when picking out the perfect outfit. At the end of the day, I think it really does come down to finding a unique sense of style that is true to you. Pay attention to trends, but at the end of the day, wear what you love and don't worry about if something is "trendy" or the "it item." For me, I tend to have a very eclectic and colorful sense of style, but that is definitely not something that happened overnight.

From a very young age, I can remember being drawn to colorful, sparkly clothing. When everyone else in my school was wearing a variation of jeans and fur-lined boots on dress-down days (not that there is anything wrong with that), I was wearing bright pinks, silver sequins, and tulle skirts that resembled tutus. And though my style was a bit whacky at times, I was always encouraged by my parents to dress myself and have fun with fashion, so I was always taking risks, even when I didn't realize it! You could say I've been working on developing my personal sense of style for over twenty years now; it really does take a long time. But when I first started my career in the fashion industry and interning in the magazine world, my style drastically changed. My maximalist tendencies often left me feeling self-conscious and out of place, and I began questioning my sartorial choices. You see, many of my coworkers came to the office day in and day out in a uniform of jeans, white t-shirts, and some sort of ultra-chic footwear (the Valentino rock stud was the shoe of choice at the time!). In an attempt to blend in with my counterparts, I began gravitating toward neutral colors and, though I hate to confess it, all-black looks, if you can believe it! I eventually realized that this just wasn't me. I discovered that I feel most confident when wearing eclectic colorful looks, especially if they contain some sort of glitz or glam. From there on out, my personal style was officially born. Each and every day, I am still experimenting and pushing the limits of fashion, and fashion week really gives me the opportunity to have fun and bring it!

During February fashion week, things are a bit different from fashion week in September since you really have to dress around the crazy and unpredictable weather. All that really matters is your outerwear, i.e., a big statement coat, or an eye-catching beanie or some really cool shoes. Fighting against the frigid New York City temperatures is hard enough, so I find that while jumping from show to show, a faux-fur statement coat is the way to go (rhyme not intended: this is serious fashion advice, people)!

My first real February fashion week was when I worked for my first magazine right out of college, and I wasn't aware of the bold outerwear (unspoken) rule. I spent so much time preparing my outfits, worrying and obsessing over them, and making sure they were perfect. But when the day of the shows came, I ended up layering a black heavy-duty warm coat over my outfits, so no one really ended up seeing my outfits anyway. All that worry and preparation was for nothing because all that was seen was my black coat! I was disappointed I didn't think to just focus on my outerwear. But, hey, lesson learned!

Walking and taking the subway is perfectly fine during September fashion week when the temperatures are 70 degrees and up. However, in February you'll be more inclined to take a taxi everywhere you go because even walking one block to the subway hurts with the winter wind, and your face becomes the color of a tomato. Try splitting a cab with friends or coworkers. This will save you money in the long run, and it's also nice to show up at an event with people rather than solo. Not to mention the potential of slipping on black ice in the winter when trying to maneuver the streets in heels, so let's just say wearing the appropriate footwear is also extremely important.

One February, I was waiting in line to get into a show. I had a ticket with a seat number, but even so, there is still always a line to get in. As I'm waiting in line, a girl walks up behind me with open-toed slingback heels and bare legs. All I could think was Are you nuts? There I am with my huge coat and two pairs of tights on and still shivering. I immediately asked her, "Aren't you cold?" She replied, "Yes, but thankfully my boyfriend is waiting right outside with a car for me, so I only have to walk a few feet outside."

Must be nice! (I yelled in my head) #goals.

For the 99 percent of us who don't have that luxury, please dress for the weather so you don't end up in the ICU with hypothermia or frostbite.

> When starting out in the industry, I would often show up to events alone, which has its pros and cons. The cons are that you might be the only person who doesn't know anyone there. You'll be forced to try and meet people and network so you're not that awkward girl standing in the corner alone. The pros are, you will be forced to meet people and network and break out of your shell! Widening your "fashion web" and connections in the industry are key. Whether you're just starting out or have been working in fashion for twenty or more years, you can never know too many people.

Whether dressing for fashion week or an event or even just a day in the office, there is one rule I always stay true to: dress for the job you want, not the job you have. Whether you're an assistant, an assistant's assistant, or an intern, you should always dress professionally to make a good impression on your boss. When it comes to fashion week in particular, though, it's even more important to dress the part because who knows who you might run into. Now, I don't mean breaking the bank on uberexpensive items, just look for statement pieces in any store you go to! Also, it's important to remember when you're

DRESS FOR THE JOB YOU WANT!

first starting out to not feel discouraged by what others might be wearing. Leading up to fashion week, editors and bloggers often borrow clothes from designers and return them after, so if you see someone decked out in head-to-toe Chanel or Gucci, it is probably on loan. Unfortunately, when starting out, you won't have the luxury of doing this. A great way to find statement pieces is by shopping at vintage stores around the City (or even in your local town). If you're not in NYC, The RealReal and Vestiaire Collective are two of my go-to online stores for finding designer pieces for a bargain. There are so many good ones, so as fashion week approaches. spend an afternoon going through the many racks of clothes. I am sure you will find a hidden gem or two! But, the most important accessory you can wear that doesn't cost a thing? Confidence. Confidence is free and can be spotted from a mile away. When you walk to and from the venues, there will be swarms of photographers waiting to capture the coolest street style for various roundups, and with confidence I'm sure one of them will lift their lenses to take your picture.

I remember the first time a photographer stopped to take my picture, I felt like a superstar. It was February 2015, the last season at Lincoln Center. It was early in the morning and I was making my way to the venue. I was wearing red plaid pants from GAP, a leather jacket from H&M, and a red scarf (it didn't have a label)! Nothing too special, but I guess it caught the photographer's eye. Being a little assistant at the time, it felt great to know someone admired my style (that was actually affordable)! When picking your shoes for fashion week, it's super important to stay comfortable or bring a pair of shoes to change into. You don't want to be remembered as the girl who fell/broke her heel/ ruined her Manolo Hangisi's. I once heard about an editor

who broke her Celine sandals during fashion week—tragic! In the winter-time, opting for a fashionable boot or something with a lower heel is most practical. February fashion weeks are usually given a warm welcome by Jack Frost himself, so trying to maneuver the streets of NYC in heels while dodging dirty snow is not a pretty picture. Personally, during September fashion week I will wear heels or fun sandals every day, but when it comes to February, statement boots, embellished loafers, and fun sneakers are the way to go.

> When going bright and bold for fashion week, you want to make sure not to overdo it. There is such a thing as the worst-dressed list, and you definitely don't want to end up on that. I once worked with this girl who always wore bright and bold pieces and she usually always pulled them off, but this one outfit in particular was just a little too much. Well, when the "worst-dressed of fashion week" article came out, her picture was the lead. I almost died for her.

When all else fails and you are still stumped in the morning with a pile of clothes by your feet, just stick with a neutral base and add some fun accessories. Black will never do you wrong, and it is the easiest color to style with some bold statement pieces. As Coco Chanel once said, "A woman without a little black dress has no future." While that does sound extreme, I do believe in the power of clothing and that fashion should be fun. Investing in a little black dress not only saves you from a headache when you don't know what to wear, but it is also a great go-to for interviews. Talk about impacting your future!

Chapter 9

FAKE IT TILL YOU MAKE IT

The winter before I graduated college, I promised myself I would attend fashion week not as an intern or volunteer this time, but as a guest. I wasn't sure exactly *how* I was planning on making this happen, but I was determined to, well, make it happen. To backtrack a bit, the summer before my senior year, I had the amazing opportunity of interning at a fashion magazine, and a month after that I was asked to style two MTV celebrities for the Video Music Awards (but that's a story for another book). Anyhow, I took what I had learned from these two incredible experiences and tried to work my way into a few shows. I started emailing a few people I had formed good relationships with while I was styling/ interning and expressed my interest in attending their shows as a, um . . . stylist. I mean, I had had that one styling job, right? So, I took full advantage of it.

> Sometimes you need to word things appropriately to get what you want. Determination is key in everything you do and especially in this industry. This can apply to your job or internship search, as well. Fashion editors and people in this industry in general receive at least one hundred emails on a daily basis (I'm not kidding). You need to do something that will make them remember you and help you stand out among a large sea of potential candidates. When I applied for my first job, I emailed editors until my fingers turned blue. Most didn't answer, but the few that did either A. knew one of

Making It in Manhattan

Thankfully, one of the contacts I made that previous summer remembered me, and the impression I left on her was a good one. She immediately offered me an invite to the show and congratulated me on my styling work. One ticket in the bag, yes! I then reached out to my old internship supervisor from my first gig, the one who I interned with again a second time for fashion week, and she was more than happy to offer me a ticket to their show, as well. Woohoo, two down! My final attempt was to reach out to an alumnus I had met through a networking event at my school. He worked as a professor at a fashion university in Manhattan and always helped put on their fashion week show at Lincoln Center. When I met him, he mentioned that I should reach out to him around fashion week if anyone from our school would want to attend the show, so when I emailed him, I not only asked for a ticket for myself, but also for the girls on the executive board of the fashion club in my college. I was the president of the club at the time, and our school was small so I figured it would be really cool to give as many students as possible the opportunity to attend. He happily obliged, so there I had it: three invites as a *guest* to fashion week! I immediately informed my professors, of course, that I would need to miss a few days of class for fashion week. This was beginning to seem like a common occurrence for me now. But, hey, I was going either way. Thankfully, I wasn't given too much trouble. I packed my things, said bon voyage to my professors, and traveled home to New York to prepare for my big week: my very first fashion week as a, ahem, stylist. On the way home, I stopped at a few stores to, of course, pick up a few "necessities," as I call them. If it's fashion week I can justify buying just about anything really. These new shoes? A new dress? A purse to match? Well, it is fashion week so . . . sold! When living and working in New York, everything seems to be more expensive than it would be anywhere else. For those of you just starting out, there is no need to break the bank when trying to look good, as I've said before. I have many shopping secrets that I could share, but my biggest one is sample sales and vintage shopping! Sample sales in New York are the gold mine. Designer fashion at half the cost—why not? One of the best places to find out when samples sales are happening in New York is 260SampleSale.com, and for sample sales online, try 6pm.com.

My first show of the season was a big presentation. At this point I hadn't actually been to a presentation before and was really excited to see what it was going to be like. A presentation is different from an actual fashion week show because the models are stationary and you are the one moving. The designers will go all out with the setting and decor to really convey their story and inspiration behind the collection. One of the themes of this particular collection was fairy tales. Anyone who knows me is aware of my love for fairy tales, so I was in heaven when I walked in and saw a model playing Snow White lying in a glass box wearing a gorgeous ensemble finished with glittery red shoes. Also, propped up on a "hill" (we were inside, though) was a model with hair trailing down to the floor. Rapunzel, of course. The venue was really big and packed to the brim with attendees, so many that at times it was even hard to make your way around without bumping into people. It was all so magical, though (the fairy-tale theme obviously helped), and I couldn't believe that I was actually there in the midst of it all yet again. As I walked around taking picture after picture and really trying to soak it all in, the designer came out to speak to press, so I got to see her, which made the whole experience even cooler. I was standing just a few feet away from the designer who put on this entire production. I quickly snuck my phone out and got a picture of her, but the person next to me wasn't as slick. One of the PR people saw and quickly instructed her to put it away followed by an "or else" face that scared me as well, even though it wasn't directed toward me. The public relations teams are in charge of putting on the fashion week shows, so during that week they are under a lot of pressure. The fate of the entire show or presentation is in their hands (their jobs are actually really cool), so they want to make sure it all goes seamlessly. With that in mind, I would try my best to listen to their instructions, follow their directions, and don't ask them for too much when you are just starting out. You don't want to somehow get on their bad side for the future when you may be communicating with PR teams on a daily basis, so it's super important to make friends and form good relationships with these people.

Soon after the designer came out, celebrities started coming out of the woodwork. I spotted Paris Hilton, who refused to take pictures with people (though I did try) and Anna Sophia Robb, who I did have the opportunity to meet. I have always been a huge *Sex and the City* fan (I mean, who isn't?), so I really admire her from the show *The Carrie Diaries*. If you haven't read the book or seen the show, I definitely recommend both.

I left my first presentation feeling like I was on cloud nine; my first show was a huge success. Unfortunately, I made a rookie mistake and didn't bring a portable phone charger, so my phone died, thankfully not until after I had gotten all of the pictures I wanted.

> With the arrival of fashion week comes a flood of social media, it's honestly hard to even keep up. Instagram especially is always blowing up with pictures, videos, and Boomerangs from shows, so it's important to make sure your phone is thoroughly charged (obviously I learned that the hard way)

or else you might miss out on the perfect photo opportunity. On top of making sure your phone is charged, always bring a portable charger or recharge-able phone case with you. Think about how many times you'll want to update your feed or send out that perfect Instagram story throughout the day. Be familiar with the hashtags and handles for each show; this way your picture will get more views should you load it with the appropriate tags. Whether you have a large following or not, a post with #NYFW will definitely bring some traffic to your page. During the week, scope out the area the venue is in. Find the nearest coffee shop, restaurants, and even the nearest tailor should you have an outfit emergency midday (you never know!).

The next day I was scheduled to attend the show for the designer I had interned with. I arrived at the venue and waited in line with the standing room ticket section once again, but now I knew better. I was practically a seasoned veteran, so when I made my way into the venue, I found an empty seat and was able to sit comfortably with my goody bag on my lap and just wait for the show to begin. The show was beautiful, as always, and I got to see so many familiar faces, which was nice because it brought back so many wonderful memories. The most familiar face I saw though was that of a six-foot bombshell. It was none other than my girl Karlie Kloss. After the show, I was able to go backstage again and see everything and everyone in action. Just a few months ago, I was one of these people full of anxiety and excitement, and now I got to just stand back and take it all in. Backstage I got to actually meet Karle Kloss, which I hadn't done last time since I was so busy prepping for the show, I knew she was tall, but wow was I shocked. Last time I saw her I didn't actually get to speak with her or stand right next to her, so I didn't get to see how tall she really is. I'm about 5'9" and I felt extremely small stand-ing next to her. As we proceeded to talk, I was able to get a picture with

her. In today's world of social media, did it really happen if you didn't get a picture?

The next day, I ventured into the city early to grab lunch with a friend before my show that evening, and she asked me if I wanted to attend a show with her after lunch. (Later on, I will go into more detail about this show and what adventures ensued.) Later that evening was the show the alumni from my school had gotten myself and other fashion students from my school into. It made me extremely happy to see my classmates there and to be able to share their first fashion week with them. To share fashion week with someone and give them the opportunity to be in the City during such a magical time felt extremely rewarding, since I could remember my first fashion week just like it was yesterday. Fulfilling my duties as fashion club president, check! To this day, my old fashion club still ventures to the City to see this show, and I love meeting up with the students when I can because I still love experiencing fashion week with someone who is going for the very first time. Nothing beats the excitement and pure happiness you can see on their faces.

That was supposed to be my last show of fashion week, so it was just about time to get my head back into reality when my boyfriend had an idea. My boyfriend hadn't actually been attending any shows with me, but he took off from school as well to partake in the excitement of just being in the City during the magic of it all. He was in the City to drive us back to school later that night when he remembered that his brother's girlfriend at the time was a model and used to work in New York sometimes. She was just starting out in the industry, but he thought maybe she had some connections? It was definitely worth a shot! He immediately called her up and asked if she could get us into any other shows that day before we had to leave. It turned out that at nine that night she was actually going to be walking in a show for a smaller designer at Lincoln Center but would put our names on the list as her guests backstage. Yes! One more show so I could hang onto the magic for at least a few more hours.

We arrived at the venue early, of course, to make sure everything was settled. She told us to come in the back entrance, which I was familiar with from my days as an intern; I was getting flashbacks of rushing to Lincoln Center carrying garment bags. When we arrived, though, things didn't really go as we had hoped. The person manning the door didn't have our names on the list because apparently it was typed before she called in to add us. She came out to the front and tried to barter with the security person working the door, but they wouldn't let us in. Another awkward encounter with a fashion week security guard to add to my diary. We were so close, yet so far. They told us we could sit backstage near the security desk, but not in the actual show. What a tease! They wouldn't let us in or say they would try to let us in at the last minute should there be empty seats. Time passed and I could tell the show was starting soon and my heart sunk. As the music began to play, I felt so defeated. I was sitting right behind a fashion show but I couldn't go in and actually watch, how awful. Just then, though, some official-looking woman with a headset (a headset makes everyone look more important) walked toward us. She obviously didn't know about our situation but came up to us and asked in a lighthearted tone, "What, you don't want to sit inside and watch the show?" I sprung out of my seat, "Um, YES, we definitely want to watch it!" She quickly brought us through a different entrance, snuck us through security, and let us stand with all of the photographers in the press pit to watch the show. All press and photographers are seated together at the end of the catwalk so they can get the best pictures for their websites, so we pretty much had the best view in the house. It's a very exciting area to be near and I couldn't believe we were there. We had made it. Not only did we get in somehow by a fashion miracle, but we now had the best view for pictures. After the show our friend who had modeled came out to apologize thinking we still hadn't gotten in, but boy did we have a story for her.

Chapter 10

TAXI, TAXI!

After my first summer internship, and very exciting winter volunteering at fashion week, I decided I wanted to experience what the editorial fashion world was really like. Upon arriving back at school, I learned that an upperclassman at my college had had a fashion magazine internship the summer when I was interning in production, so I decided to ask her to coffee and see what she thought of the experience. She happily agreed, and I was thrilled to hear what she had to say. During our coffee date, I was honestly a bit disappointed when she told me how awful her internship experience was and how it completely turned her off from the magazine world. Though this was a bit disheartening to hear, I decided I still wanted to learn for myself, so after our coffee date the upperclassman kindly shared with me her supervisor's contact information, and I eagerly ran back to my dorm room to compose the perfect email.

> It's important to take advantage of your resources. Whether you're still in college or graduated and working, take advantage and use the resources that are around you. Similar to my "never take no for an answer" mantra, I also have to stress, always experience something for yourself. Just because one person had an unfortunate internship experience doesn't mean yours will definitely be the same.

How to Properly Format a Résumé

I remember when I was a sophomore in college and getting ready to apply for my first internship that summer: my résumé was awful. It was cluttered with activities I had participated in when I was in high school, none of which were relevant anymore. In an attempt to salvage my weak résumé, I went to the learning center at my college to revamp and resuscitate it to try and land an internship. In the hopes of helping you land an internship, dream job, or make a career change, here is how you should properly format your résumé.

Most important, keep things simple, clean, and concise. The more white space the better, because it will make your résumé easier to look at. An employer will only spend a few seconds looking at your résumé so it's important to make sure their eyes know where to go. Practice by looking at your current résumé and seeing where your eyes go first. Even practice this with a friend, give them a copy of your résumé and ask them where they look first. Does their eye go to your most important experience? Or do they get lost in a clutter of bullet points? Keeping things clean and simple will guarantee your employer can easily make their way around your résumé and get a sense of who you really are. When listing every experience you've had, I would limit yourself to maybe three or four bullet points under each one. There is no need to write a novel; that will just waste your space and make your résumé look messy. These bullet points should give your employer just a taste of your experience; the full meal will come once you land an interview.

When it comes to the length of your résumé, unless you are a director or editor-in-chief with decades of experience, it should *not* be more than one page! Editing your résumé down to one page makes it easier to look at. With this and my above points in mind, you are ready to actually start writing your résumé!

To Begin

Start with your name centered at the top of the page in a larger bold font. Underneath put your email address, phone number, and mailing address. Keep the font of your entire résumé consistent and choose one that is classic. I don't suggest Comic Sans MS (even though it's fun). I'd stick to Times New Roman or Arial.

Next

Include a section called "Relevant Experience" where you can put any experience you have that relates to the job or internship you are applying for. For example, if you're applying for an internship with a fashion magazine, I would list any other fashion internships or writing experience you've had. I would also list your school's fashion club/magazine if you are an active member. When you are starting out, your résumé is probably going to feel a bit bare; I know mine did. Especially when I was applying for my very first internship, I felt like I didn't have anything to put on my résumé. So I ended up listing my college's fashion club and magazine and talking about them a bit. I also listed a job I had at a small boutique as a sales associate—anything helps!

After That

Include a section with any other work experience you have or college activities that you are involved in but that might not necessarily be related to fashion. I would call this section "Campus and Community Involvement." In this section I used to list the sorority I was in, any charities I volunteered for, the cross country and track team I ran for in college, as well as other jobs I've had, like the time I was an ocean lifeguard. Though this job isn't related to fashion in any way, it shows that you are responsible and can be trusted with important tasks.

Chapter 10 | Taxi, Taxi!

At the Bottom

Feel free to list your education either at the very top right under your name or at the bottom. When starting out, I used to list it at the top but have since moved it to the bottom. I would call this section "Education" and list your college and expected degree and graduation year. I don't feel it is necessary to list your GPA unless you really would like to.

> The traditional cover letter is not as important as it once was in the fashion industry. The body of the email is your new cover letter, so make that count. Your future employer will probably only take a few minutes to look over your email, so put your most important information right at the top.

After sending out my résumé, the next day I heard back from the internship coordinator, who asked me if I would be able to come in for an interview. Leading up to the interview, I tore my closet apart in the hopes of finding the perfect interview outfit. (Looking back, I would have never worn this outfit now, but I guess at the time it worked.) I wore a long maxiskirt in mustard yellow (similar to the color of barf), a white sweater on top, a chunky gold necklace, and gray T-strap heels. This was at a time when the topknot was very popular, so I tied my entire outfit together with a big topknot on my head. I probably looked very cute and trendy, but now this wouldn't be something I'd necessarily wear to an interview. The reason I say this isn't because the outfit wasn't interview appropriate; it most definitely was at the time. But it's just not necessarily my style anymore. Yes, I have since retired my topknot. That being said, I often get asked how formal to get for an interview, and my answer to that is, it really depends on the company. I mean, you should always look polished and put together, i.e., no jeans. But, I think what you might wear when interviewing for a job at a bank as opposed to what you might wear to interview for a job at Betsey Johnson is completely different.

Making It in Manhattan

Being that I'm from New York and grew up in Staten Island, the day of my interview I gave myself plenty of time to commute into Manhattan. My interview was at 12 pm, so I got on the ferry at 9:30 am. The office was located in midtown west, so my plan was to take the ferry downtown and jump on the subway, which would take me close to the office—sounded simple enough. Since I figured my trip would be seamless, I got all decked out and even wore my heels. I have since learned wearing flats and changing into your heels upon arrival is much easier (and more comfortable) when you have a longer commute.

When I got off the ferry, though, my trip was not as easy as I had hoped. My typical subway entrance had been shut down due to flooding from Hurricane Sandy, which had happened just a few months prior, so when I got off the ferry, I really did not know where to go. I wasn't very familiar with the City at the time, and honestly I began to panic. I turned to a few other people who had just gotten off the ferry, and they instructed me on the best train to take, which they swore would take me to the building. The train took forever, though, since it was one of the only ones running at the time, so I'm not going to lie, I was definitely getting nervous and kept checking the time on my watch. When I got off the subway, I did not recognize my surroundings at all. I'm the kind of person who always asks a lot of questions, so in this case, I thought it necessary to ask someone where the heck I was! I peeked my head into a small café and told one of the workers the address I needed to get to and asked where that was in regard to my current location. They informed me that I was on the east side and had to get to the west side. There were no subways I could take there, so I began to walk—in my heels. As the minutes passed and I began to sweat knowing I might be late, I figured I only had one other option.

I had to take a taxi.

I had never hailed down a cab before, but the image of Carrie Bradshaw doing so in *Sex and the City* time and time again flashed through my mind. So I thought to myself (or we could say WWCBD, what would Carrie Bradshaw do?), just channel your inner Carrie and it will all work out. *Gulp.* I mean, it had to. I couldn't be late for this interview. The odds of getting an open cab weren't very high, so to this day I say the fashion gods must have been with me, because sure enough an open taxi came my way after only a couple minutes of frantically standing on a street corner. I hailed it down in a way that I knew would have made Carrie proud.

As I jumped in the cab, all I could stutter out was the address followed by, "Please get me there before twelve!" My driver could sense the urgency in my voice and thankfully zipped up 57th Street as fast as he could with traffic. With ten minutes to spare, I checked in at the front desk of the building and began to make my way up to the interview. I think I was on such an adrenaline high from my whole almost-being-late fiasco that I didn't even have time to be nervous or overthink the actual interview.

> *Always and I repeat **always** budget yourself extra time when going to an interview. In my case, I had no idea of the events that would transpire and my almost being late. Thankfully I had given myself an ample amount of time to get there; otherwise, I might not have gotten the internship and probably wouldn't be writing this book right now! Also, always play it cool. When I got up to my interview and met with my future employer, she asked, "How was your commute from Staten Island?" Instead of telling her my long tale, I simply replied, "Oh, it was easy, no problem at all." I knew she wouldn't really want to hear about my problems, and it would only take time away from her actually getting to know me and hopefully (fingers crossed) hiring me.*

Making It in Manhattan

My interviewer proceeded to ask me about myself, my past experiences interning, and why I now wanted to work in editorial. I had done a lot of research on the magazine, so I was able to proudly list examples of features I loved and how I wanted to be a part of it all. I also made sure to mention my classmate who had interned there and she thankfully remembered her, so it was a good thing I had name-dropped.

A few days after the interview, I got an email offering me the internship. Commence the internal happy dance! My career path in editorial was soon beginning. So once the summer rolled around, I made sure to do a test run to the building a few days before I started. I definitely did not want a repeat of my interview fiasco on my first day. (I think something was deleted that shouldn't have been, so I added this back in).

And as far as what I learned from all of this, especially after attempting to power walk several avenues in three-inch heels, always bring a spare pair of shoes in your purse.

Chapter 11

THE SNEAK ATTACK

I hate to admit it, but I have done the unthinkable. I've shown up to a show and snuck in without a ticket *and* ended up sitting front row! The fashion week show I previously told you about when I went as a "stylist" is the same one I snuck into with my friend who I mentioned I met up with for lunch. My friend went to college in the City and was interning for a blogger at the time. Interning for a blogger during fashion week is like the Holy Grail, especially if it's a blogger who doesn't live in New York and doesn't want to make the trip up; bloggers might only want to make the trip to New York to attend the bigger shows (especially if its February and freezing), so interns are (most likely) given the other tickets! Getting invited to fashion week, even if it is a smaller show, you always want to go or send someone in your place to build a good relationship with the designer and their team. So my friend was extremely lucky and got to attend a ton of shows in her boss's place.

I remember being in my friend's apartment with her an hour before one of the shows at Lincoln Center. Her boss had emailed her an invite, and she started convincing me she could get us both in with one ticket! Believe me, I was skeptical, and believe me, I was terrified of getting in trouble, but there is just nothing like attending a fashion show, so after a lot of her reassuring me we would be fine, I was in.

Our plan sounded super simple: we would print out two copies of the same ticket (yes, that's when people actually printed their tickets and didn't just scan them on their phones). She would walk in first and I would walk in a few minutes behind. Her ticket would scan but mine, of course, would not since it had already been used, but security would just think the scanner was acting up and let me in. Sounded like the perfect plan at the time, but nothing ever goes as planned in life, especially when you're running on a New York City high (and not necessarily thinking clearly). Something was bound to go wrong with our half-baked plan.

When we first showed up at Lincoln Center, all was going well. My friend walked up, scanned her ticket, and went right in, then a few minutes later I strolled up with the second copy. I tried my best to act confident, like I wasn't doing anything wrong, except when I scanned my ticket, security wasn't as ready to just let me in as we had thought they would be. I was

faced with many questions. "What's your name?" "Are you sure this ticket hasn't already been used?" "Who are you covering for?" *Gulp.* My heart was racing. I thought, *Is there such a thing as fashion week jail*? Because if there is, I was totally going to end up in there. The key, though, to the whole plan was to play it cool and really act like I belonged there and wasn't doing anything wrong. Pretending like you're meant to be there rather than like you got caught is usually the best option. Thankfully, it was only a few minutes until show time and they were being bombarded with other problems, so I was able to slip through the cracks when my friend walked out and exclaimed, "Oh, there you are!" and just dragged me in through the crowd. Amid the confusion, no one said anything—we were in!

Inside the venue was really dark and my friend's ticket was slated for front row. I didn't really have a ticket, so I asked her where I should stand. She convinced me to just sit next to her in the front row and play it cool, easier said than done, obviously. I don't think there was any way I could really "play it cool" with the thought of getting in trouble at fashion week (of all places) racing around in my mind. As more and more people poured in, I was freaking out that someone was going to confront me and take me to "fashion week jail," unglamorous mug shot and all. When the PR people running the show walked by, I just kept my head down hoping they wouldn't notice me.

Finally, after what felt like an eternity, the lights dimmed and the show started. I had made it, I was sitting in my first front row seat at New York fashion week. (Please don't pinch me this time, I never want to wake up!) The show was incredible and made even sweeter because I was front row, and, oh, did I mention there were gift bags?

Full disclosure: I am *not* recommending you sneak into a fashion show because 1. I've never been so nervous/anxious/sweaty in my life, 2. I don't want you getting into trouble, and 3. Earning your ticket in feels one thousand times better because there is nothing like knowing you are supposed to be there. (But, I will say it proved to be an incredible experience and a really good story to tell.) A few months later, a short video came out recapping the show. Lo and behold, whose faces were in the background? My friend and I were spotted on film! *Ha.* To this day I still talk about our "sneak attack" and how far we've come since then.

Chapter 12

PLEASE GIVE YOUR NAME AT THE DOOR

As time passed and I graduated college (no more ditching class for fashion week), I landed a job as a fashion assistant at a magazine. Fashion assistant roles vary at different magazines, but I was blessed with truly amazing bosses who helped me really push myself and learn so much about the industry.

I started working with them halfway through September fashion week, so my first season with them wasn't too eventful. I only attended a couple of shows since I was somewhat new and thrown into it all, but I'll never forget the first show I covered on the magazine's behalf. I showed up at the front desk and checked in under the magazine's name and was immediately greeted by friendly faces and very kind people. They were probably just being super nice to me since I was with the magazine, but I wasn't going to question it. It was a very small show, but I was placed right in the middle of the front row! Hey, front row is front row no matter what show it is (and I didn't have to sneak in this time: I was actually supposed to be there!). Before the show began, I was approached by a photographer from Getty Images who wanted to take my picture at the show. I happily obliged and gave them my name and title at the time: fashion director's assistant. Lo and behold, a few days later the photo was posted to Getty Images and stated my name and underneath it my title, which read Fashion DIRECTOR! Oh boy, they forgot the assistant part; thankfully no one said anything, but I definitely had a good laugh about this with my friends.

When fashion week rolled around in February and I had been with the company for several months now, my bosses were absolute saints and allowed me to attend so many shows. This was February 2015 and what I would call my first real NYFW. Running from home to a show to the office to a party and back. It all sounds very glamorous, but is also extremely tiring. And I loved every single second of it.

As a fashion assistant, on top of attending the shows, I was also in charge of doing the scheduling, ticket requests, and travel arrangements for our editors for not only New York fashion week, but also for the London, Milan, and Paris shows. I had a lot on my plate, but I was more than up for the challenge. I had had experience in requesting tickets, since I had done it for myself in the past, so that was easy enough. When managing someone's schedule, you have to make sure you are very organized (you don't want to leave your boss in a foreign country with the wrong show information), so I created Excel spreadsheets for every fashion week with the proper show information, their confirmation status, as well as a contact the day of the show. For the duration of New York fashion week, I arrived at work early, checked all of my emails, updated the schedules, and attended a few shows daily. Fashion week in New York is honestly the most insane time of the year. (By insane, I mean completely awesome, but insane nonetheless.) It's the one time of the year where you'll be in the same room or sitting next to the likes of Kanye West, Whoopie Goldberg, Kim Kardashian, as well as, of course, Anna Wintour. The key to all of this, as I said, is playing it cool and acting totally normal. "Oh, that's so-and-so celebrity? I hadn't noticed." Freaking out will just get you weird looks, while going up and introducing yourself and starting a casual conversation will feel surreal and a memory you'll want to write down. (Like I'm doing here.)

This February fashion week was one of my most memorable because not only did I get to attend so many shows, but I also sat front row for

99 percent of them, since I was attending on behalf of the magazine. When you're covering a show for your boss, though, and sitting front row for them, there is something you should know. I was attending a show at good old Lincoln Center. It was a show for a designer I wasn't too familiar with, but during fash-

ion week I attend pretty much every show I am invited to because I love seeing the clothes and taking in the atmosphere and excitement. This show in particular I was covering for my boss, so I was told to give her name at the entrance. I wasn't given any trouble and was told where my seat was right in the middle of the front row. I casually walked over to my seat and started getting ready to sit down. As I walked over, though, there was a girl standing near me in the second row who looked confused—too confused.

> Look as though you belong and were supposed to be there or you could be questioned or even kicked out. As I said, always dress the part and act professionally. The best idea when starting out (or when sneaking in) is to blend in, which is super easy to do during fashion week given the amount of people there.

I don't know the full story, but apparently this girl was covering for her boss, as well. When asked for her name, she gave her own name, not her boss's name—big mistake. Now she had this big PR woman, whom I'll call Jane, yelling at her, saying, "Front row is for editors only!" *Gulp.* I just put my head down and began reading the program. Thankfully I was fine and no one gave me a problem, but jeez, I felt so bad for that girl. What a way to start your day.

During this fashion week I had the pleasure of sitting across from Kanye West, a few seats away from Whoopie, and near the rapper 2 Chainz. I would have been next to him, but someone had taken my seat. But, being that I have done the deed and snuck into a show I wasn't supposed to be at, I usually never call anyone out if they are in my seat, so I happily took another seat in the venue.

I remember I was sitting in the front row of a show I was covering for my boss when Whoopie Goldberg came in with her granddaughter and things got a bit crazy. The front row was filling up quickly: I think people were just sitting there to be close to Whoopie and the PR people wanted to make sure the row wasn't too crowded and that everyone who was actually supposed to be front row was. PR person Jane again was in charge of handling this show, and she started going down the row asking for everyone's affiliation, you could tell she was on a mission to catch someone and throw them out. When she got to me, I could tell from the look in her eyes that she thought I was very young. I was there for the magazine, though, so I gave their name, and she instantly replied, "Oh, okay you're fine." She was about a year too late if she was trying to catch me sneaking into a show.

My favorite celebrity encounter of all of fashion week that season was with Ashley Benson from the show *Pretty Little Liars*. I will admit it, I was a huge PLL fan, having watched from day one, and really had to keep my cool with this one and not blurt out, But who is A?! I was covering a show for one of my bosses later that evening. It was a show that I really wanted to go to, so I was ecstatic that I was given the opportunity. When I arrived, I promptly gave my boss's name and was escorted to the front row in the center. When I arrived to my seat, though, there were security guards standing right near my section. I was pretty confused but thought nothing of it. Soon after, one of my colleagues arrived and sat next to me. As soon as he sat down, he asked, "Do you know anything about the show *Pretty Little Liars*?" I of course responded "Yes," thinking Yes, I know everything and have been a fan since day one, now what's going on? Soon out of the corner of my eye Ashley Benson a.k.a. Hanna Marin arrived. I was in complete shock. They wanted to sit her next to us for a "photo op" to get some cute pictures for our site. I started making small talk with her like it was no big deal, and she was so incredibly nice. It's so nice when you meet a celebrity who is real and down-to-earth. When the show began, it was a little difficult to actually focus on the fashion with her sitting beside me. The show was over before I knew it, but before she left I was determined to get a picture. I mean, I had to show my sisters, since they love *Pretty Little Liars*, as well; word of mouth wouldn't have been enough in this case. As we stood up to say goodbye, teen girls started swarming, of course, so she was trying to make a quick exit. I asked for one quick picture and she was happy to oblige, and after our snapshot she darted out. In conclusion, that was probably the coolest fifteen minutes of my life up to that point.

Chapter 13

LEAVING A LEGACY

Once you do finally realize your love for the fashion industry or any field you wish to pursue really, there is usually something or someone that has inspired you. For me, aside from support from my family and my addiction to *Project Runway* and *Sex and the City*, there was one designer who made me really fall in love with this industry. I can't remember how old I was exactly, but I know I was very young when I first discovered Betsey Johnson. I remember seeing a girl in my school wearing a floral pleated dress one day and going up to her eager to know "Who designed that dress?" She proceeded to tell me it was Betsey Johnson, and from that moment on I was hooked. When I got home that night, I borrowed my dad's computer (an old desktop computer that now seems ancient) and went straight to Google. I searched and searched, thinking, *Who is Betsey Johnson?* All I could think was, if someone could make a dress like that, then she must be pretty spectacular. That night, I read articles, listened to interviews, and even watched any runway shows of hers I could find online—the minute I saw her cartwheel down the runway I was in love. As a kid growing up with dreams of working in fashion, after I discovered Betsey Johnson all I could think was that she was a direct reflection of the fashion industry, and if working in fashion is this much fun, then I have to be a part of it. Having her as a driving force in my life really helped me never lose sight of my fashion dreams and was one of the biggest reasons I decided to pursue a career in this field.

To put it simply, Betsey Johnson doesn't play by the rules. She designs what she wants, what she loves, what she wants to see in fashion, and

that is what makes her stand apart from
the rest. This aesthetic is what I love.
Watching her designs twirling down
the runway behind my computer screen
made working in this industry seem like
a dream. It made it feel like each day was
a new adventure, a new opportunity to

do what you love, and that's when I knew what I had to do with my life.
Have fun and pursue something I love.

> *I've heard it said that if you love what you do, you never truly work a day
> in your life. I think this is one of the most important things you can carry
> with you throughout your life, to love what you're doing and enjoy each day.
> Life is way too short and too busy to get caught up or stressed out about
> the little things.*

As I got older, I slowly built up a collection of jewelry, bags, shoes, and
clothing from Betsey Johnson, and each time I wore one of her designs I
felt closer to my dream of working in this industry. Her designs are also
what helped me stand out from the pack wherever I went, since they were
always bright or bedecked with a fun pattern.

I went to college in a very small town, which was the opposite of my
hometown in New York, so I was a bit out of my comfort zone. When
everyone would show up to class in their sweatpants and oversized shirts,
I would show up in a pair of sequin boots or an oversized faux fur coat (I
mean, someone had to). As cliché as this may sound, I made sure that each
day, even if I was going to go sit in a biology class, I dressed my best. You
never know who you might be running into, whether on campus or out

in the real world, so it's important to always put forward your best version of yourself. Plus, knowing my luck, the one day I would decide to "dress down," I'd run into someone important.

Always be yourself. In a world full of pigeons, be a flamingo. In other words, don't always play by the rules. Don't always stick to what is "trendy" at the time. Follow your instinct, what you like, what makes you passionate, and just go for it. Just because everyone else is wearing jeans and fur-lined boots doesn't mean you have to. It's so important to stay true to who you are as a person because that is what makes you special and makes you different from everyone else. When you go on an interview, wearing something that exemplifies your personal style will often help you stand out in a sea of candidates. I personally always start with a really good pair of shoes!

Finally, during my junior year of college, I was presented with an opportunity to meet Betsey Johnson after having looked up to her for years. Aside from being extremely excited to finally meet the woman who inspired my love for this industry, I was also very nervous. What if she wasn't what I had hoped her to be? What if instead of fun-loving and easygoing (like she appeared online), she was actually the complete opposite? I feared that my dreams and my spirit might be a bit crushed, but it was a risk I had to take. I was determined to finally meet my fashion idol, so during my spring break, instead of taking a crazy trip to Cabo or Miami, I ventured into Manhattan to see my idol set up a window display at a major department store. The day of, I got decked out head-to-toe in her designs. (I mean, is there any other way to dress when meeting a designer than to wear their designs?)

I arrived early and quickly began networking with girls on her team. It turned out the event was just to watch her set up the visual display, not to actually meet her, unfortunately (sigh). But, as I've said before, I'm a very determined person when it comes to things like this, so as I networked with her team, I made sure to express my interest in possibly meeting her after the event. They told me that they would see what they could do, but that is never something to get your hopes up for.

The event lasted several hours, and as people came and went to watch her through the glass window, a few others and myself stayed the entire time, excited to see the finished product and just to be in the presence of Betsey herself. As the event started to come to a close, I was feeling pretty discouraged that I would most likely not get to actually meet her. I tried to tell myself that at least I got to see her in person and that was enough, right? But before I could even finish convincing myself not to be disappointed, I was approached by someone who told me to follow them into the store, so I quickly did before she could change her mind. They led me through the department store and into a back room where I was finally given the chance to meet my idol. Walking up to her I was extremely nervous but was instantly calmed when she told me she had wanted to meet me all day after spotting me through her display. She noticed I had stayed during her whole presentation and also that I was wearing one of her designs (it did pay off!). She turned out to be everything I had hoped she would be and only reassured me of my career path and to keep following my dreams.

Fast-forward about two and a half years from that moment, and I was now working at a fashion publication writing for their digital team. Aside from getting to report on trends and give style advice, which is what I love to do, I was also given the amazing opportunity to occasionally interview designers and celebrities, so I was able to interview Betsey several times now and get to know her on a more personal level. When fashion week rolled around in September of 2015, this designer's show was coincidentally coinciding with her fiftieth anniversary as a designer, so I instantly jumped at the opportunity to interview her for such an important occasion. I immediately pitched the idea to my boss, and once it was approved I started planning out my outfit. Not only was I getting the chance to meet my favorite designer yet again, but I was also going to be attending her show at New York fashion week. Though I had been following her career for some time and had watched almost every single one of her shows online, I was never able to actually attend one of her shows in person and was more than excited.

The day of the show, I arrived at the venue two hours before show time. Backstage was everything I could have hoped it would be. From hand-drawn notes to the models from the designer herself, to a DJ, and bottles of pink champagne—this was a full-on Betsey Johnson party. When my time came to interview her, she herself was definitely emotional. Even big-time designers with more than fifty years in the business still get preshow jitters. She described the collection as her "last segment," starting with her clothing now and then going back in time and ending with what she believes was her inspiration to become a designer, her dance costumes. She compared her show to a dance recital, and I could definitely see the similarities. From the countless hours of preparation and planning, this was in fact her performance time. And what better way to top off her performance than with her dance teacher (who was now 94 years old!) attending the show.

To be sitting backstage prior to one of fashion week's biggest shows with Betsey Johnson herself was a moment I will forever cherish. After years of studying her designs and hoping to make my way in the industry, this was definitely a big moment for me. Before I left, though, one of the biggest questions I had to ask her was for advice, advice she would give to aspiring designers but also fashion hopefuls alike. She replied, "Love it, be prepared to work hard, have some talent, and love it, really love it. Somehow you

will have your dream and you will do it!" There is no better advice in life than just that: love what you are doing. It is never too late to reinvent yourself or to start off on a new path. So what if you originally thought you wanted to become a teacher or a scientist but now realize that just isn't for you? The fashion industry isn't going anywhere. It may be changing and evolving, but it surely isn't dying. It is here for the taking if you seize the moment. Since that interview, I have never forgotten her words. There is no such thing as "luck." If anyone tells you, "Oh you're lucky you got that job," kindly reply, "Luck didn't have anything to do with it." You worked hard, proved yourself to the employer, and truly deserve this opportunity. Once you are given the opportunity, though, you must be prepared to work hard, give it your all, and never look back.

> As far as "leaving your legacy" goes, I can't speak from experience in this realm because I haven't yet left a legacy. What I can say is that I have been in the presence of designers, editors, and models who have left and are continuing to leave a legacy on this industry. Though all of these people are very different, they all have one thing in common: their love for their careers and their passion and drive to make it in the industry. They all at one time or another had a unique vision or a dream and decided no matter how hard things might get that they would never let anything stand in their way.

Chapter 14

PEACOCKING

As I've said, my first real full-fledged running-around-the-city-to-shows fashion week was when I was an assistant at a fashion magazine right after I graduated from college. At that point, I didn't truly understand the concept of "street style" or why photographers gathered outside each show. In February when it's cold and even potentially snowing, all that matters is your outerwear and shoes. A really cool oversize statement coat and crazy colorful pair of pumps (closed toe, of course) or boots, and you're pretty much every street-style photographer's dream. I didn't really get that memo my first jam-packed fashion week, and I focused so much on my outfits that stayed hidden underneath a very warm but black coat. Nobody really saw what I was wearing underneath, so I didn't get photographed as much as I would have liked. Well, one year later, I was now working at a different magazine on the digital fashion team, and I was excited to try this whole street style thing again.

I decided to make the switch over from the print side of magazines to the digital side because digital was (and is still) becoming such an important aspect of the industry, and I wanted to give it a try. I was still working for a fashion magazine, just playing for a different team, I guess you could say.

As time passed and fashion week approached, I started mentally preparing my outfits in my head and definitely bought a statement coat (or two!). But aside from stepping up my wardrobe and trying to look the part, I wanted to be able to act the part and look like I knew what I was doing behind the camera. I reminded myself that when all else failed to just have confidence and no one would assume I wasn't a pro. Pretend you know what you're doing and people will (hopefully, fingers crossed) believe you (i.e., fake it till you make it!).

The proper term used for what I was about to try out is *peacocking*. When you type peacocking into Google, its definition is to "display oneself ostentatiously; strut like a peacock."

From my understanding, peacocking is standing outside in front of the photographers and #WORKINGIT! Looking cool and confident, walking toward the shows and then stopping to strike a pose, letting many photographers take your picture. The more who take a picture of your looks, the better, because then you are more likely to be featured in a street-style roundup or style story. When you're starting out in the industry, you're going to be faced with a ton of well-established editors, bloggers, and even celebrities who all have impeccable taste, so getting noticed can be tough. But this fashion week, despite the  odds, I was determined to have my picture taken and make it into one of those style roundups. After much research and trial and error, here are my seven tips for dressing like a street-style star:

HOW TO DRESS LIKE A STREET-STYLE STAR DURING FASHION WEEK

1. Plan out your outfits the night before or a few days before the show so you're not scrambling that morning. (I now even plan a whole week in advance!) You'll want to give yourself time to try everything on to make sure everything fits and that your outfit looks good together. Sometimes the look you pictured in your head doesn't look as good in real life as you imagined it would, speaking from experience, so planning out your outfit a few days in advance always helps.

2. Investing in a few statement items is key. Whether a coat, dress, or pair of sequin pants, it helps to find one item that will really pop to be the main focal point of your look. These pieces do not need to be super pricey, though! Look at Zara, H&M, and Topshop—they always have great items that are more affordable. If you're in New York, try hitting up a sample sale or two.

3. Find a pair of shoes that are comfortable but also chic. You're going to be walking (or running, if you're late) around the City to shows all day long, so it's best to wear a pair of shoes that won't cramp your toes or give you blisters. Or if you're dying to wear your four-inch strappy colorful shoes, bring a comfortable pair to change into while commuting around the City.

4. For February specifically, dress in layers. You'll want to opt for a fun statement coat, but underneath your statement coat wear a turtleneck, sweater, and maybe even another lightweight jacket. It can get really cold out there (and usually for some reason always snows during fashion week), so be prepared.

5. Accessories are key! Not sure what to wear? A fun hat, cool pair of glasses, or eye-catching purse can really be all you need to create a unique look. A hat is always a great accessory because just in case you oversleep and are having a bad hair day (we've all been there), it can

still help you look polished and pulled together. And during February when it often snows, a cool beanie or beret will cover up any snow-covered hair situation you may have going on.

6. Denim is your friend. With the right styling, you can wear jeans to fashion week. You may be thinking, *But aren't jeans too casual?* In fashion, it's a really "anything goes" kind of mentality. Wear with a cool graphic tee or patterned blouse for a street-style-ready look. Or wear a simpler top and find a pair of denim with some cool embellishments, fringe, or DIY with vintage patches!

7. Most Important: make sure your bag is stacked with all of the essentials, e.g., subway card, phone charger, business cards, a snack—it's going to be a long day.

When the first day of shows finally arrived, I was more than excited? Ready? for fashion week to begin. On my first day, I had three shows and wanted to look my best to kick things off. Now, as I've said before, there's no need to go out and break the bank; I personally love mixing both high- and low-priced pieces. My entire look was an eye-catching cobalt blue (I like to think this color is my power color) and very photographer, friendly.

A "power color" is what I call my best color. The one color I feel most comfortable and confident in and one that I feel suits my skin tone best. For me, mine at the time was a royal/cobalt blue. It often changes and is sometimes a bright pink or red.

I started my look with a pair of blue-and-white Old Navy pants—yes, Old Navy! I told you I shop high- and low-price points. I then paired these pants with a structured white vest from Topshop that has fringe around the bottom (you barely saw it, though, because it was under my jacket) and layered it over a Uniqlo turtleneck so I wouldn't freeze. To top my look, I wore a blue striped faux fur coat from Boden (on sale!). I was a bright sea of blue that day. Accessories are key, so I paired my look with my favorite pair of blue Manolo Blahnik Hangisi pumps but wore them with a blue sparkly sock. (You may be thinking, *This girl is crazy, socks with Manolo's?* But I swear, it looked good.) Now, I'm not going to lie, I don't know anyone who can wear heels all day let alone run to fashion shows in them, so to budget my time in pumps, I brought a pair of sneakers with me. You may be thinking, *Where did she keep these sneakers?* Well, I used two bags: one tiny purse and a larger clutch. In the clutch I put a small pair of Keds that I was able to easily slip on and off during my downtime, so I was fully prepared for the day ahead and ready to take on NYFW in stride, literally.

For a day full of shows, it's always important to keep your purse stocked. Below are my essentials for surviving and thriving!

10 Things I Always Keep in My Purse during Fashion Week

1. Wallet (of course!).

2. Business cards: Leading up to fashion week, especially if it's your first time attending, business cards are a great thing to have on hand. Fashion Week *is the* time to meet as many people as possible and to network within the industry, so as you're meeting people and mingling, it's important to have a solid business card to hand out.

3. Portable phone charger so you don't miss a beat.

4. Mints: Gotta keep things fresh!

5. Mini makeup bag for touchups.

6. Snacks: During the day you could go hours without a real meal, so keeping some snacks on hand will help curb your appetite and keep you from getting hangry.

7. A change of shoes to give your feet a break if you're wearing heels.

8. Hand warmers: I used to use hand warmers all the time when I ran cross-country in college, but they are actually very helpful during fashion week. When it gets really cold out, put them in your coat pockets to keep you warm.

9. Advil/Aleve/Tylenol: In case you get a headache or if your feet start to hurt.

10. Glasses/Sunglasses: If you're like me and can't see anything that's farther than ten feet away.

My first show of the day was at 10 am, so I arrived at the space at around 9:40. Shows usually never start on time and usually run about 30 minutes late, so there's no need to stress if you aren't there right on time. As I got out of the cab and prepared to walk toward the venue, I was instantly flooded with emotions (happy, anxious, nauseated—not sure if you'd consider that last one an emotion), but above all very eager for the week ahead. But I was also nervous about being photographed. My goal this season was to attract the attention of street-style photographers, so I was crossing my fingers (and toes) that my outfit would do just that. But with getting noticed you also run the risk of ending up on the worst-dressed list. That's where my nausea kicked in. If that happened, I had no idea what I would do. But, hey, if you don't put yourself out there and try, you will never know!

I turned the corner facing the new-ish fashion week location at the time and took a deep breath. As I walked down the street, I instantly felt like I was walking down a runway. Photographers were lifting their cameras and I was fully prepared. I even got asked to stop and pose to allow photographers to get their "perfect shot," which allowed me to really show off my peacocking skills that I had practiced in my bedroom mirror. The experience was a bit overwhelming since I'm not usually photographed while walking down the street in New York, but it definitely made me feel really good, and like I had done something right. After that experience, and having photographers gather around to snap every single angle of my look, I came to the conclusion that fashion week gives regular people like you and me the opportunity to live like a celebrity for a week and feel what they feel. The "paparazzi" of NYFW are very eager and not afraid to chase you down for a picture. And I can assume that that's what it is like for celebrities but about one thousand times worse. But for that week, it makes us feel unstoppable. You always want to make sure your outfit, as well as hair and makeup, are on point, so by the end of fashion week you are usually pretty drained, at least I am. To look camera-ready every day, I always wake up early to go the extra mile on my hair and makeup, which I definitely do not do every single day for work.

A few days later, my fashion week adventures continued, and my street-style quest was still in full swing. Two days in, the temperatures had drastically dropped, and I was trying to adjust my outfit choices accordingly. This was the Saturday of New York fashion week, so I thankfully didn't have to actually go to the office at all, but that also meant I'd be out in the field going to shows all day, so I had to wear a very warm and comfortable outfit. I hadn't worn denim yet, so I wore a pair of cutoff cropped jeans from 7 For All Mankind. I paired my jeans with a chunky gray sweater from C/MEO and my studded Miu Miu sneakers (got these for an awesome deal). On top of my sneakers I added faux fur pom-poms and a glitter silver sock (of course) to keep my ankles warm. To top my outfit I wore a pastel pink coat (the color of the year at the time according to Pantone, Rose Quartz), a jeweled beanie, and an emoji cross body bag to tie it all together. So my outfit was very "street style"-ready but also super comfortable and warm.

I was making my way to my first show of the day when a photographer stopped me and asked to take my picture. I was thrilled (doing my inner happy dance)! As I'm standing there posing (which probably looked hysterical since I was freezing but still trying to look cool and confident), I saw a man pop through the sea of photographers wearing a bright blue jacket, and I had to do a double take. It was

none other than the legendary Bill Cunningham, *the* street-style photographer. My jaw almost hit the floor. As I tried not to stare, he walked over to where I was posing and started taking pictures of me, as well. Insert very happy and shocked emoji face here.

Bill Cunningham was a fashion photographer who worked for the *New York Times* but was widely known for his cobalt blue coat, riding his bike around Manhattan. He is recognized as the originator of street-style photography, so you can imagine I was in awe when he stepped up to take my picture. As I posed for Bill, I tried to look as experienced as possible. After all, he's photographed every well-known fashion personality and editor you could think of.

After that day, I rushed home to check the *New York Times* to see if Bill had by chance posted my picture. The picture never did surface, unfortunately, but I'll never forget that moment—my ultimate peacocking moment, if I do say so myself!

As fashion week continued and I proceeded in my attempt to strut my stuff for the street-style photographers, I realized that my mission was overall successful, even if I didn't end up in any street-style roundups. I now knew what it took to get the photographers to notice you. Bright colors and bold pieces always do the trick, but it's definitely not as easy as it looks when it's below freezing outside.

At this point I hadn't achieved my one goal, though, which was to be included in a street-style roundup. I tried to tell myself that I had given it my best effort and I always had next season to try again. Toward the end of the week in between shows, I headed to the office to get some work done and saw an email at the top of my inbox with the subject line "YOU GO GIRL" with a link. At first, I feared it was spam or some sort of virus, but I figured it wasn't my personal computer so might as well see what it was. As I clicked on the link, it brought me to a street-style roundup, and as you can imagine, my jaw hit the floor. IT WAS ME! I had done it, I was in a "See the Best Looks from Fashion Week" article—I had done it! Right in there with some of my favorite bloggers like Leandra Medine from Man Repellar and Jacey Duprie from Damsel in Dior as well as countless editors, there was little old me with a big cheesy grin on my face.

Chapter 15

I'VE GOT A GOLDEN TICKET

You may be wondering: New York fashion week sounds so fabulous but how do I actually get in? How do I get a ticket? Volunteering with a designer is a good way to start. Now, I'm not going to lie: volunteering during this exciting and busy time won't be easy. It will probably consist of long hours and a lot of hard work, but in the long run it will look amazing on your résumé and be well worth it.

Another way to land that coveted ticket is to intern for a blogger. If this blogger feels they can trust you, he or she will (most likely) give you tickets to shows they themselves cannot attend. When attending in place of your boss, take full advantage of the opportunity. Make it a point to talk to as many people as you can and network as much as possible.

The season I attended fashion week as a stylist was only my senior year of college, so you might be wondering how I got my invites. I started by going through contacts I had made at my internship as well as doing some research and finding the proper email addresses for various PR companies online. When emailing PR teams to try and get an invitation to fashion week, it's important to make yourself sound professional. When starting out I didn't know what to say exactly, but over time and through trial and error I learned. These teams receive so many ticket requests leading up to fashion week, so it's important to get yours into them earlier rather than later. If you are requesting a ticket on your own behalf and not in accordance with a publication, they might not be as willing to give you a ticket, especially if you are reaching out to them at the last minute. To put in an official ticket request with the PR companies, I suggest using my email format below.

FASHION WEEK TICKET-REQUEST EMAIL

Subject: (insert designer's name here) NYFW Ticket Request

Dear (insert PR person's name here),

I hope you are doing well! My name is (insert your name here), and I would love to attend your upcoming show this (September/February) at New York fashion week. I am currently a (blogger, stylist, consultant, editor—explain a bit about what you do and include any relevant links to your work) and would love the opportunity to see your newest collection live this season.

Thank you so much for your time and consideration. I look forward to hearing from you soon.

All my best,
(your name)

When you're first starting out, you will probably get a lot of rejections from companies saying they cannot accommodate you this season, but don't let that stop you. I always say it can't hurt to ask and you're no worse off than you were before if they say no. At least at that point the company knows who you are and can potentially keep you in mind for next season.

Chapter 16

WHAT TO DO IF YOU DIDN'T ATTEND A BIG FASHION SCHOOL

When it came time to go to college, most people assumed I would choose a school in the Big Apple. Since I grew up in Staten Island right outside of Manhattan (and yes, it is a New York City borough!), it seemed only natural that's where I would go to pursue my love for fashion. But, when it came down to it, I actually decided to do the complete opposite and get out of New York for college. Just like Dorothy Gale in *The Wizard of Oz*, I wanted to experience something outside of my own backyard. I wanted to branch out, meet different people, and just experience living in a place other than where I grew up.

Going to a big fashion school as opposed to a "regular college" (what really defines a regular school these days?) has its ups and downs. Most people finishing high school and getting ready to take the next big step into college must face this decision. If you know you want to pursue fashion but aren't quite sure which realm of the industry you're interested in or even if you just don't know 100 percent if it is for you, you might be torn with your college decision.

PROS & CONS OF GOING TO A BIG FASHION SCHOOL

Pros

- You will be in one of the biggest fashion cities in the world.

- You will have the opportunity to form very relevant connections.

- There will be more internship opportunities near your school.
- You will have time to learn your way around the big city and see if living in such a fast-paced place is really what you want.

Cons

- You won't get a typical "college" experience (football games, Greek life, etc.).
- You won't have the opportunity to live on a big campus.
- You won't meet many people going into different industries.
- If you change your mind about studying fashion, you may have to change schools.

> *As you can see, there are two sides to every coin. It's extremely important to make a decision that is best for you and that will ultimately make you happy. Life is way too short to not put yourself first when it comes to a major life decision like choosing a college!*

Aside from my desire to actually get out of the City (I don't know who I was back then because now I *love* Manhattan), I was actually a runner all of high school and wanted to continue to pursue that in college, which was part of the reason I decided to go to a small liberal arts college in Pennsylvania. I really enjoyed my experience there, but I was lucky that on summer breaks I always had the option of going back to my home in New York and was able to intern in the City.

> For anyone who grew up in some part of New York, we refer to NYC as "the City" since it's the city we grew up with. Since I am from New York, I will often refer to Manhattan as "the City," but I was once having a conversation with someone and they kept saying "the city," so I assumed we were both talking about NYC until about halfway through the conversation they told me they weren't talking about NYC at all. They were talking about Philly! To clarify, when I say "the City" I mean NYC!

I know personally from my own experiences and from friends I went to school with that no matter how much you love your school, it can sometimes feel discouraging being outside of Manhattan and as though there are not as many opportunities or résumé boosters at your fingertips. Here, I am going to break down how to work toward your career goals and your dreams even when you're not at a big fashion school in the City.

BREAK OUT OF YOUR SHELL

Freshman year when I went to college, I was a social butterfly when it came to my personal life. I went out of my way to get to know almost everyone in my dorm and took time to make as many friends as I could. When it came to what really mattered, my fashion classes, I was the complete opposite. My first year, I was actually very quiet in all of my fashion seminars and didn't make much of an effort to raise my hand or comment in our lectures. I was mainly just trying to absorb as much as I could and take it all in, but I was actually very nervous. To me, I felt like everyone else must know so much more than I do about the fashion industry, so in an attempt to not embarrass myself, I didn't say too much.

Thankfully, about halfway through my freshman year I met some upperclassmen in the fashion department who were extremely welcoming and helped me become more confident in myself. Slowly I started feeling more passionate about my classes, and finally I decided to join my school's fashion club. This was definitely a turning point in my life. Joining this club taught me so much about myself and about working with others. It taught me how to work in a creative, collaborative, and fun environment and see my work come to life.

> One of the best pieces of advice I have ever been given was "What do you get out of being shy?" My sister told me this when I was about fifteen, and it completely changed my outlook on life. In high school I was pretty introverted, and after she told me this I went out of my way to make an effort to talk to people, which is why I made it a point to go out of my way and meet as many people as I could in college. When starting college, remember this: what do you get out of being shy? The answer: nothing (in my honest opinion). College is a time to take advantage of every opportunity that comes your way and to try new things, so try your best to break out of your shell, try something new, and say **yes** to as many new opportunities that come your way. This advice has also been helpful in my career because now at every and any event I go to I am always the first one to introduce myself and form new connections.

GET INVOLVED

Come my sophomore year of college, I made an effort to get more involved on campus. Between becoming more active within our fashion club and holding an executive board position, I also became a writer for our school's fashion magazine. The more involved you become in your major during college, the more experience you will gain and the more you will be able to put on your résumé. You will also meet a great group of people and ultimately build a pretty solid network, which can help you down the road when applying for jobs.

Now you might be saying, "My school doesn't have a fashion club." If that is the case, my biggest advice would be to create your own! How cool would it be to be one of the founding members of your school's fashion club? The probability of having other students at your school who are also interested in fashion or some sort of creative field is very high. Go out of your way to find those people. Tell them about your idea to start a club and go from there. There is no better feeling than creating something and watching it grow. Creating your own fashion organization will help you build strong leadership skills and networking abilities. You will be forced to go out of your way to meet people and speak with faculty members to help get your club approved as a school organization. Make this your passion project and don't stop until you achieve your goal. If your school already has a fashion club, take full advantage of it, just like I did! Become a member and learn the ropes. Ask the upperclassmen in the club about their lives, internships they've had or currently have, what path of the industry they hope to pursue, etc.

> _It's extremely valuable not only to make friends within your own class, but also to make friends with the upperclassmen in your department. These students will have already taken the classes you are in and can truly help guide you through the next four years (and hopefully down the right path). They will be also be leaving college before you and entering the workforce sooner, so by the time you are ready to graduate, these friends could be a great resource when you are job hunting._

WORK FOR YOUR SCHOOL MAGAZINE

During my sophomore year, I also became a writer for our fashion magazine, and it actually helped me figure out what I wanted to do with the rest of my life. Before joining, I never even considered fashion writing as a career. Could something so fun actually be a thing? I didn't think it was possible. When I attended  the first meeting, I didn't really know what to expect. I mean, I had flipped through the pages of *Vogue*, *Elle*, and *Marie Claire* hundreds of thousands of times, so I figured this could be something I might be good at. After the first meeting, I was hooked and really formed a love for writing. Being in our pitch meetings was extremely inspiring, and I loved the fun and collaborative environment we shared. I never really considered myself a "writer" before I joined this club and really doubted my abilities, so I can't stress enough to take a risk like I did. As time passed I eventually became the student editor-in-chief of this publication my senior year and was always trying to recruit new writers. The one hesitation I was always met with was that these people didn't think they could write. Just because your history teacher in seventh grade told you that you were a bad writer because you were bored out of your mind writing your paper (this happened to me), you are not necessarily a bad writer. When you are faced with the opportunity to write about something you are actually interested in and are passionate about, that will show through in your work. And, hey, even if you don't want to become a writer one day, this will **A.** be good practice at showing you what you don't want to do, **B.** give you a better understanding of fashion, and **C.** teach you how to properly talk about different trends and even how to properly pronounce designers' names (super important!).

If you are still a bit hesitant and don't necessarily want to join a school paper or magazine, creating a blog is always an option. I am not saying to start your blog with the intention of becoming the next Blonde Salad (love her!), but rather do it as a creative outlet. Use your blog as a place where you can write about anything you want. In the crazy world we live in, having something you can call your own and something you can just do for fun and that you are passionate about and get excited to work on is always so important.

> When you graduate college, creating a portfolio to showcase your work is an easy way to show you are organized and will also help your future employer see how serious you are about a career in this industry. It's proof that you actually did something productive over your past four years of college other than partying. Not sure what to put in this portfolio? Well, what about all of the great articles you wrote for your school fashion magazine or pieces you styled for the magazine? There are so many aspects that go into producing a publication. Approach the leaders of your school magazine with your ideas and I am sure they will be thrilled you are so passionate and interested in participating and will welcome the extra help!

TAKE ADVANTAGE OF ANY OPPORTUNITIES PRESENTED TO YOU

No matter what city you live in, there is always some way you can get involved with the fashion community there. Whether it's working at a small local boutique or volunteering your time at a clothing drive, these are all great ways to get involved that are still relevant to fashion and offer good experience you can put on your résumé when first starting out. When I decided to really step things up in college and get involved, I took advantage of everything that came my way. This was a time when I had not yet had any internships, so I was looking for ways to gain experience within my surroundings that would make me a better candidate for a future internship. I also didn't have a car on campus, which made my options a bit limited, so I got to thinking, *how could I possibly gain some "work related experience" on campus?* I then had a "light bulb moment" (those are my favorites) and thought, Why don't I see if I can assist within my own fashion department at my college?

Once I got that idea, I excitedly headed over to the fashion building to speak with the head of my department. I went to her office and explained my interest in becoming a departmental assistant, and she was thankfully all for it. The job didn't pay much, which I was totally fine with because it allowed me to gain some great experience. I spent most of my time creating Excel spreadsheets (which are super helpful to know when going into fashion; I used them all the time at my first job) with alumni contacts and also organized our magazine shelves. Anything they needed, I was their girl. Finally, I had something somewhat substantial to put on my résumé, and I was thrilled. Plus, it gave me some incredible one-on-one time with my professors that was truly invaluable. I'd often sit down with them to see how they thought I was doing and brainstorm possible ideas for our fashion club and magazine. This job was really an outlet for me that helped me escape my day-to-day life on campus, and since I've left, the fashion department at my school has taken on several other assistants. Approach your professors and ask them if this might be something you could do. It never ever hurts to ask; the worst thing they can say is no!

PLAN A FASHION SHOW

During my senior year of college, I was in charge of curating our student-run fashion show. Each year the fashion students would put on their own show in the fall and it was my turn to step up to the plate and I was more than a bit nervous. But, I have to say, being in charge of planning a fashion show was an incredible experience that taught me so much and helped me to really respect and admire designers and PR firms that put on shows several times a year; it's not as easy as it looks! There is just so much that goes into a fashion show other than making garments. As students we went into the task a bit blindly, but in the end, it was such a rewarding project, from working with the designers and consulting with

them along the way to securing a location, locking down a date, deciding a theme, sending out invites, and praying people actually would attend. There was a lot to do. I can remember a few days before the show having a meeting with all of the designers and models to decide on the order of the show, which was more difficult than I thought it would be. Especially working with students and around everyone's busy schedules, it was a bit chaotic. Especially since I wanted to have my hands in a little bit of everything and make sure the show was absolutely perfect, I had to learn the beauty of delegating tasks and not trying to micromanage and oversee every little thing. The things I learned in planning this show I have taken with me into my career now, and they have all helped me excel in my current career.

STAY CURRENT

Though you may feel like you are a million miles away from Manhattan, which you actually could be, a very easy way to feel connected to everything that is going on is by staying up to date on the latest news, events, and fashion shows. I love looking at Women's Wear Daily, fashionista. com, fashionweekdaily.com, whowhatwear.com, as well as reading every fashion magazine I can get my hands on so I can stay up to date with breaking news in the industry as it happens. During fashion week, I am always refreshing voguerunway.com to check out the latest shows. Doing your research and staying connected is so incredibly important. Also, when you start going on interviews for a job or internship, your employer might ask you what fashion sites you read, so it doesn't hurt to actually do some research and know what you're talking about.

TAKE TRIPS

Whenever your schedule might allow, take a trip to New York City. When you have a break from school, make it a point to come out to the City and explore. There is nothing like being in the middle of all the excitement and magic in the city; it is really just a realm of opportunity. Like Taylor Swift says, "It's been waiting for you!" Too cheesy? Nah.

Chapter 17

WELCOME TO NEW YORK

There's no time like the present to start making connections and building relationships. As I've said before and can't stress enough, network, network, network. Networking is the key to making it! Before you even start your job or internship quest, I suggest planning a trip to New York City, which is, in my opinion, the mecca for all things fashion; nowhere better to begin your journey. But before you take your trip, there are a few things I would suggest.

Make the most of your time while in the city. Use your social media resources and try reaching out to people in the industry you admire. Write them a short email or direct message like I outlined earlier (pg 10). Keep your message short and sweet and ask them if they might be willing to meet you for coffee or even an informational interview. An informational interview is not an interview for an actual job. It's an interview for you to come prepared with a load of questions to learn more about a particular company and employer's career. If you're just starting out, informational interviews will help you not only build vital connections within the industry, but will also help you learn if a certain career path is for you. These interviews obviously won't give you the hands-on learning an internship can provide, but they will help you skim the surface and learn more about how a company works and could ultimately help you land an internship. I suggest setting up as many informational interviews as possible to help grow your network. Who knows, you could end up bonding with one of the people you meet and down the road they could keep you in mind when they hear of a job opening.

Take advantage of all that New York has to offer. Visit museums, walk the High Line, visit Central Park, go shopping in SoHo, and if you don't mind crowds, you could even take a walk around Times Square.

Getting to learn the subway system prior to your first internship in New York is super helpful, as well. During my first few internships, I was often asked to run errands, and whether it consisted of getting someone's lunch or picking up a sample from a design house, knowing how to use the subway made my life a whole lot easier. Personally, I feel the subway looks scarier than it actually is and just takes a bit of practice before you truly get it down. I can't tell you how many times I accidentally ended up on the west side when I was supposed to be on the east side or uptown when I was supposed to be downtown. Just like interning and learning about the industry from your hands-on experience each and every day, learning the subway is similar in that each day you are riding it you are getting better acquainted with it. I will admit I still sometimes get lost, so when running errands around the City or even just going to meet friends after work, Google Maps will become your best friend.

Chapter 18

HOW TO TURN YOUR SIDE HUSTLE INTO A FULL-TIME BUSINESS

With the rise of social media, becoming your own boss has become a very doable thing. With top bloggers and influencers making six-figure salaries every year, it has to make a person think. Can I too become my own boss? Can I turn my side hustle into a full-time job? These were the two questions I asked myself repeatedly over and over again in my head—sort of like a broken record that I didn't want to stop. I wanted it to keep playing over and over again until it became too loud for me to ignore, and it did. So eventually, I had to listen. But before you go out and leave your nine-to-five job like I did, there are a few things to keep in mind when really trying to turn your side hustle or your passion into a full-time gig. Or, as I like to say, leaving your "dream job" to pursue your dream. Because honestly, life is too short, and there's nothing worse or more frustrating than working a job that you're not passionate about or having regrets.

First things first: start dedicating as much time as possible to the project. That means every day after work, on your lunch break, and most definitely on weekends. This is your free time away from your everyday job, so use your free time to really hone in on the project and make it the best it can be before pursuing it completely. This could mean passing on after-work drinks with friends or a Saturday brunch, but in the end you have to think to yourself, *How badly do I really want this?* The more time you put into it now, the easier it will be when it comes time to make the transition. Yes, you will have to make sacrifices, but *yes*, it will be worth it. The best advice I can give you before leaving is to test the waters out a bit. By that I mean see if the product you have will actually sell or get your blog up and running before you leave and see if people are actually reading it. While still in the comfort of your job, and steady salary, try to test it out and see if you can indeed make money off of it. If you come back and realize yes, I can actually make money off of this,  off of something you love, then my advice is to take the plunge. Personally, I'm a "there's no time like the present" kind of girl. I knew I wasn't getting any younger, so eventually I just took a leap of faith.

Once you do step out on your own, make it a huge priority to network. Schedule coffee dates with former colleagues, bosses, and even friends. The more you spread the word of your new venture, the more likely you are to succeed. You never know, someone you meet with could connect you to someone they know who could completely change the future of your company for the better. And don't, I repeat, *do not* be afraid to talk your business up! It is your baby after all, so don't be afraid to share the major things you're doing and accomplishing.

No one is going to believe in you more than you are, and no one is going to stand up for you more than you are, so don't be afraid to speak up for yourself and know your worth. More often than not, I'm asked how much I would charge someone for a certain service. That is always a tough question, it's become easier over time, but in the beginning, I honestly had no idea how much money to ask for. And I also never wanted to scare someone off because I thought my work was worth more than what I was being offered. Always know your worth and do not settle. In the long run, people will respect you more for that.

I can't really remember the moment I decided I wanted to become my own boss. With that being said, I didn't just leave my job right then and there and pursue my side gig. I actually ended up waiting about a year and change before taking the plunge. Although that time waiting for the moment to come was difficult, I'm thankful for that time because I used it to take everything I was learning in my current position and applying it all to my passion project. That is what really helped me become successful, using what I was learning in a more corporate environment and applying it to my little start-up.

Eventually, the voice in my head telling me, "DO IT—LIVE YOUR DREAMS!" became so loud that I had to listen; I'm sure if you have a similar moment you can clearly remember it as well, and the feeling of relief when you decided, this is it. I'll never forget the moment I gave my notice that I was leaving. Even though I liked my job, I was so incredibly passionate about my side hustle that deep down I knew it was what I had to be doing. It felt like a weight had been lifted off my chest when I walked out of the office. I felt confident in my decision, but there was still a tiny voice in the back of my head saying, "Are you sure you want to do this?" She's since quieted down.

Chapter 19

ONE PIECE OF ADVICE

As crazy as our day-to-day lives can be, I always think it's important to take time to just sit back and reflect on the things you've been through and be proud of what you've accomplished. Whether it's after your first semester of college, your first internship, or a few months into your first job, it's nice to look back and see how far you have come and think about where you hope to go down the road. I am a firm believer that in life everything happens for a reason; you might not know what the reason is at the time, but it will all work itself out in the end. I wouldn't say I necessarily have any regrets or things I wish I had done differently, but if I could go back and give myself one piece of advice to help me through this journey, it would be always to stay true to myself.

There are already so many talented and stylish people out there, but there is only one you. Figure out what makes you, well, you, and run with it. No one can take your individuality or unique sense of style away or make you change who you are. I wouldn't say I've ever necessarily lost who I am, but I have had moments where I've definitely questioned myself. One of them in particular was back during that February fashion week when I was trying to work on my street-style game. Like a lot of us, I love having fun with fashion. For this particular day of shows, my office was closed and I didn't have any shows until the evening. When I woke up in the morning to get ready, it was freezing, as it always is during February fashion week, and they were even predicting snow later that night. In the early afternoon it did unfortunately begin to snow and the streets were an absolute mess, so in view of the horrible snowy weather and the fact that I only had one show, I decided to keep my look warm, comfortable, and cute. I wore a fun denim-on-denim look a.k.a. a Canadian tux. I paired my look with these cool bright pink sneakers I had recently gotten, a very heavy royal blue parka to keep warm, and a fun printed neckerchief (a small handkerchief you tie around your neck, similar to a ban-

dana). It definitely wasn't one of my fanciest outfits, but it was laid back yet fashion forward, and perfect for the horrible weather I was about to face outside. As I made my way toward the venue, I was happily surprised when I was approached by photographers yet again. I let them snap a few shots and then headed into the show, since I couldn't bare being outside in the cold. As I walked into the venue my ticket was for the second row and I took off my parka and grabbed my seat. I don't know if it was because of the horrible weather or if people were just worn out by then, but the show wasn't filling up, so a few minutes before show time the PR team was instructing people to move up and fill in seats, and I was thrilled I was able to move into the first row. There is nothing like sitting front row at a fashion show and getting to see the clothing up so closely that you can really see the details. It's an incredible experience being able to take it all in in the heart of the show. The woman who was sitting next to me in the front row wasn't as thrilled about my movement, though. She proceeded to turn and tell me I wasn't "dressed to sit in the front row." I will never forget this moment because up until then I'd never really questioned an outfit I'd worn or felt like I had made a bad fashion choice. Not to mention she was wearing snow boots! Nothing against snow boots, but you could imagine I was a bit offended by her comment since I was excited about my little denim on denim pairing. She proceeded to tell me I should hide my sneakers because they weren't fancy enough and even asked me to switch seats with her since mine was one spot closer to the beginning of the runway, which I did, in shock and disbelief. By this point my face was flushed red and I was absolutely embarrassed and wanted to just crawl into bed and hide. Since she was much older than I was, I stayed quiet and tried to tell myself that I looked fine and that fashionable sneakers are, well, fashionable. (I kept repeating this mantra in my head to try and ease the pain.)

I can honestly say I had never been in a situation like that before when someone accused me of being underdressed. I am always someone who overdresses and loves wearing wild and crazy outfits, so her comments hit me hard and started to make me question what I was wearing even though throughout fashion week I had seen tons of people wearing sneakers. I continued to try to reassure myself mentally that I was not in the wrong, but the whole encounter left me feeling very defeated. As I said, I didn't say anything back to her because I like to always try and put my best foot forward and truly do believe that karma will (and does!) catch up to people, so I just sat there and tried to focus on the show and the exciting surroundings I was in, while at the same time proceeding to eye everyone else's footwear.

Later on, when the show ended and I began to gather my things and dart for the door to head home so this nightmare could be over, she turned and asked me where I worked. I felt like I was being asked a trick question or something, but I answered anyway and told her the publication I worked for at the time. It was then when I responded that her face changed from harsh and cold to apologetic. Her tune completely changed, and she then started apologizing for what she had said to me earlier. At this point, I couldn't help but laugh to myself and let it just roll off my back because the whole thing was pretty ridiculous in retrospect, and I'm sure she doesn't even remember saying these things to me now. Probably because I looked so young at the time, she couldn't have imagined I actually worked for a magazine. That is why I will repeat again, be nice to everyone!

My moral of the story is to always stay true to who you are, be confident in yourself, and always be kind to others, no matter how awful to you they may be. It would have been super easy for me to jump back at her with a mean comment about her snow boots, but instead I held my tongue and can proudly say I was the bigger person in the situation. As I've said before, this industry is a tight-knit community, so it's important to be kind to everyone.

That whole encounter made me question my quirky and eclectic style, but I've now come to realize that it's so important to stay true to who you are and your style and not to let anyone cloud your judgment, no matter how harsh their comments may be. I am all about turning a negative experience into a positive in life, and after that fashion week I just decided to step up my colorful style even more. Aside from what I have in my closet, the best accessory you should put on each morning, other than a smile, is confidence. Whether you're wearing a $5 or $5,000 dress, if you don't have confidence, you might as well be running around the City in your birthday suit. And no matter where your journey in this industry may take you, I've realized that confidence can take you further than anything, so be ready to work hard, stay confident and kind, and *always* follow your dreams, no matter how icy the New York City streets may be. As I turn the page of this chapter, just like you, I am still striving toward my end goals in the fashion industry. Stay tuned; the next best chapters of my journey, and yours, are still ahead.

13 Things I've Learned (So Far) Working in the Fashion Industry

1. Be Determined

When I gradated college, I had my sights set on working for a major fashion publication, but after several months of numerous emails and interviews, I still hadn't found a job. Thankfully, I didn't let this get to me or use it as a reason to throw in the towel. Think of everything as a stepping stone, and remember, everything happens for a reason.

2. You Have to Love It

In September 2015, I interviewed Betsey Johnson before her Fall/Winter 2016 show at fashion week, and she told me, "you have to love it." And she is so right.

3. Don't Forget to Be Humble

Remember the feeling you had walking through the doors on the first day of your internship and keep that with you for the rest of your career. You never know where the people you encounter will end up, so it's important to build good relationships and to be kind to everyone.

4. Never Be Afraid to Speak up

At my first internship, I worked in-house in the production department for a women's wear designer and was eager to learn as much as possible. After several months into the internship, I asked my boss if I could assist in a few other departments. My boss was thrilled that I wanted to take on more responsibility and started giving me more important assignments because she knew I was capable and cared.

5. STAY TRUE TO YOURSELF

Why blend in when you can stand out? Find out what makes you different and run with it!

6. ALWAYS DRESS TO IMPRESS

You never know who you could run into on any given day, so always dress to impress. That doesn't mean dressing in $1,000 labels. You can always find great pieces from more affordable brands like Zara and Topshop, vintage stores, and sample sales.

7. IT'S NOT ALWAYS GLAMOROUS

During your first few internships or jobs, you will probably be asked to take on the more administrative task, but no matter what you're doing, do it to the best of your ability. If you're making copies or getting coffee, do it with pride!

8. NETWORK, NETWORK, NETWORK

Going into my junior year of college, I decided that I wanted to intern with a fashion magazine over the summer. Though I didn't know anyone who worked at a magazine, I was determined (see rule #1) to break in. That's why I made it a point to network with an upperclassman in my school who had interned at a magazine. Always take time to meet people and learn about their experiences; you never know where it could lead.

9. Do Your Research

When it comes to interviewing, you want it to be clear that you know your stuff. If you want to work at a magazine, be sure you actually read the magazine. If you want to work for a designer, be able to reference their last few collections.

10. Don't Be Afraid to Follow Up

After an interview, you should always send a thank-you email as well as a handwritten note. If you don't hear anything after that, feel out the situation. Think about your past interactions with your interviewer to determine if you should follow up again; I always say that after a week or two, sending one last follow-up message will show your persistence.

11. Always Write Things Down

At my first magazine internship, I always kept a notebook on hand in case my boss asked me to do something. The absolute worst thing you can do is to forget to do a task for your boss, whether it is booking a car or taking down expense receipts.

12. Smile and have a Positive Attitude!

No one wants to hire the girl with a bad attitude.

13. You Don't Always Have to Know Someone

When I was growing up, I didn't know one person in the industry, so don't let that stop you from following your dreams. Always be persistent and keep your goals in mind.

ABOUT THE AUTHOR

Caroline Vazzana is a fashion editor, stylist, consultant, and founder of the fashion and lifestyle website MakingManhattan.com. She founded her site as a way to give back and shed light on the industry to the future fashion generation.

Growing up in Staten Island, New York, Vazzana always had her sights set on the fashion industry in Manhattan. In the summer of 2012, she landed her first internship with Anna Sui and then went on to intern at *Marie Claire* magazine. In the summer of 2014, Vazzana landed her first "real job" in the industry working at *Teen Vogue*. She then decided she wanted to learn more about the digital side of the fashion industry and went on to work at *InStyle*, where she came up with the idea for *Making It in Manhattan*, the future name of her editorial site and this book and an outlet to share her career advice stories and to get her readers engaged and excited.

Today, aside from running MakingManhattan.com, Vazzana is also involved in a wide range of social media brand collaborations and campaigns where she's able to lend her unique eye, voice, style, and message to the brands. She has styled celebrities for various red-carpet events such as the MTV Video Music Awards, The Tony Awards, and Comicon. Having started her career in the editorial world, Vazzana still loves fashion journalism and continues to contribute to a wide variety of digital sites.

Vazzana is often referred to as a modern-day Carrie Bradshaw.

For more fun in NYC, follow along with Caroline at @cvazzana and at MakingManhattan.com.

ACKNOWLEDGMENTS

I probably own every fashion book ever made, so to add one of my own to the mix is quite surreal. It feels as though there were so many people to thank when it comes to this passion project, *Making It in Manhattan*, so what better place to start than from my beginning?

To my mom and dad: thank you for your love, encouragement, and for believing in me since the day I was born, even when I didn't believe in myself.

A huge thank-you to my siblings, Kathleen, Virginia, and Thomas; none of this would be possible without you. It's your love and admiration that keeps me working harder and harder each day.

To my grandparents Carol and Peter, who have never missed a dance recital, soccer game, or track meet; thank you for supporting me on yet another journey.

To my grandparents Marie and Tom; though you weren't here to see my fashion dreams become a reality, I always feel your presence, and for that I am endlessly thankful.

To my other half, Dave Lopes, who's listened to me, encouraged me, and comforted me throughout this entire process and so much more—I love you.

To my literary agent, Julie Gwinn of the Seymour Agency, who believed in this project even before I fully did; I could have never done this without you.

Acknowledgments

To my publisher, Skyhorse, and editor, Nicole Mele: thank you for encouraging all of my ideas and creativity and making things I didn't even think were possible a reality.

A very special thank-you to my followers, for without you none of this would be possible.

A final thank-you to everyone who has inspired me throughout my career: my past bosses, coworkers, designers, publicists, photographers, and anyone who has touched my life along the way.